The Ghetto: A Very Short Introduction

VERY SHORT INTRODUCTIONS are for anyone wanting a stimulating and accessible way into a new subject. They are written by experts, and have been translated into more than 45 different languages.

The series began in 1995, and now covers a wide variety of topics in every discipline. The VSI library currently contains over 650 volumes—a Very Short Introduction to everything from Psychology and Philosophy of Science to American History and Relativity—and continues to grow in every subject area.

Very Short Introductions available now:

ABOLITIONISM Richard S. Newman
THE ABRAHAMIC RELIGIONS
   Charles L. Cohen
ACCOUNTING Christopher Nobes
ADAM SMITH Christopher J. Berry
ADOLESCENCE Peter K. Smith
ADVERTISING Winston Fletcher
AERIAL WARFARE Frank Ledwidge
AESTHETICS Bence Nanay
AFRICAN AMERICAN
   RELIGION Eddie S. Glaude Jr
AFRICAN HISTORY
   John Parker and Richard Rathbone
AFRICAN POLITICS Ian Taylor
AFRICAN RELIGIONS
   Jacob K. Olupona
AGEING Nancy A. Pachana
AGNOSTICISM Robin Le Poidevin
AGRICULTURE Paul Brassley and
   Richard Soffe
ALBERT CAMUS Oliver Gloag
ALEXANDER THE GREAT
   Hugh Bowden
ALGEBRA Peter M. Higgins
AMERICAN BUSINESS HISTORY
   Walter A. Friedman
AMERICAN CULTURAL
   HISTORY Eric Avila
AMERICAN FOREIGN RELATIONS
   Andrew Preston
AMERICAN HISTORY Paul S. Boyer
AMERICAN IMMIGRATION
   David A. Gerber
AMERICAN LEGAL HISTORY
   G. Edward White

AMERICAN NAVAL
   HISTORY Craig L. Symonds
AMERICAN POLITICAL
   HISTORY Donald Critchlow
AMERICAN POLITICAL PARTIES
   AND ELECTIONS L. Sandy Maisel
AMERICAN POLITICS
   Richard M. Valelly
THE AMERICAN
   PRESIDENCY Charles O. Jones
THE AMERICAN REVOLUTION
   Robert J. Allison
AMERICAN SLAVERY
   Heather Andrea Williams
THE AMERICAN WEST Stephen Aron
AMERICAN WOMEN'S HISTORY
   Susan Ware
ANAESTHESIA Aidan O'Donnell
ANALYTIC PHILOSOPHY
   Michael Beaney
ANARCHISM Colin Ward
ANCIENT ASSYRIA Karen Radner
ANCIENT EGYPT Ian Shaw
ANCIENT EGYPTIAN ART AND
   ARCHITECTURE Christina Riggs
ANCIENT GREECE Paul Cartledge
THE ANCIENT NEAR EAST
   Amanda H. Podany
ANCIENT PHILOSOPHY Julia Annas
ANCIENT WARFARE Harry Sidebottom
ANGELS David Albert Jones
ANGLICANISM Mark Chapman
THE ANGLO-SAXON AGE John Blair
ANIMAL BEHAVIOUR
   Tristram D. Wyatt

THE ANIMAL KINGDOM Peter Holland
ANIMAL RIGHTS David DeGrazia
THE ANTARCTIC Klaus Dodds
ANTHROPOCENE Erle C. Ellis
ANTISEMITISM Steven Beller
ANXIETY Daniel Freeman and Jason Freeman
THE APOCRYPHAL GOSPELS Paul Foster
APPLIED MATHEMATICS Alain Goriely
ARCHAEOLOGY Paul Bahn
ARCHITECTURE Andrew Ballantyne
ARISTOCRACY William Doyle
ARISTOTLE Jonathan Barnes
ART HISTORY Dana Arnold
ART THEORY Cynthia Freeland
ARTIFICIAL INTELLIGENCE Margaret A. Boden
ASIAN AMERICAN HISTORY Madeline Y. Hsu
ASTROBIOLOGY David C. Catling
ASTROPHYSICS James Binney
ATHEISM Julian Baggini
THE ATMOSPHERE Paul I. Palmer
AUGUSTINE Henry Chadwick
AUSTRALIA Kenneth Morgan
AUTISM Uta Frith
AUTOBIOGRAPHY Laura Marcus
THE AVANT GARDE David Cottington
THE AZTECS David Carrasco
BABYLONIA Trevor Bryce
BACTERIA Sebastian G. B. Amyes
BANKING John Goddard and John O. S. Wilson
BARTHES Jonathan Culler
THE BEATS David Sterritt
BEAUTY Roger Scruton
BEHAVIOURAL ECONOMICS Michelle Baddeley
BESTSELLERS John Sutherland
THE BIBLE John Riches
BIBLICAL ARCHAEOLOGY Eric H. Cline
BIG DATA Dawn E. Holmes
BIOGEOGRAPHY Mark V. Lomolino
BIOGRAPHY Hermione Lee
BIOMETRICS Michael Fairhurst
BLACK HOLES Katherine Blundell
BLOOD Chris Cooper
THE BLUES Elijah Wald
THE BODY Chris Shilling
THE BOOK OF COMMON PRAYER Brian Cummings
THE BOOK OF MORMON Terryl Givens
BORDERS Alexander C. Diener and Joshua Hagen
THE BRAIN Michael O'Shea
BRANDING Robert Jones
THE BRICS Andrew F. Cooper
THE BRITISH CONSTITUTION Martin Loughlin
THE BRITISH EMPIRE Ashley Jackson
BRITISH POLITICS Tony Wright
BUDDHA Michael Carrithers
BUDDHISM Damien Keown
BUDDHIST ETHICS Damien Keown
BYZANTIUM Peter Sarris
C. S. LEWIS James Como
CALVINISM Jon Balserak
CANADA Donald Wright
CANCER Nicholas James
CAPITALISM James Fulcher
CATHOLICISM Gerald O'Collins
CAUSATION Stephen Mumford and Rani Lill Anjum
THE CELL Terence Allen and Graham Cowling
THE CELTS Barry Cunliffe
CHAOS Leonard Smith
CHARLES DICKENS Jenny Hartley
CHEMISTRY Peter Atkins
CHILD PSYCHOLOGY Usha Goswami
CHILDREN'S LITERATURE Kimberley Reynolds
CHINESE LITERATURE Sabina Knight
CHOICE THEORY Michael Allingham
CHRISTIAN ART Beth Williamson
CHRISTIAN ETHICS D. Stephen Long
CHRISTIANITY Linda Woodhead
CIRCADIAN RHYTHMS Russell Foster and Leon Kreitzman
CITIZENSHIP Richard Bellamy
CIVIL ENGINEERING David Muir Wood
CLASSICAL LITERATURE William Allan
CLASSICAL MYTHOLOGY Helen Morales
CLASSICS Mary Beard and John Henderson
CLAUSEWITZ Michael Howard

CLIMATE Mark Maslin
CLIMATE CHANGE Mark Maslin
CLINICAL PSYCHOLOGY
    Susan Llewelyn and
    Katie Aafjes-van Doorn
COGNITIVE NEUROSCIENCE
    Richard Passingham
THE COLD WAR Robert McMahon
COLONIAL AMERICA Alan Taylor
COLONIAL LATIN AMERICAN
    LITERATURE Rolena Adorno
COMBINATORICS Robin Wilson
COMEDY Matthew Bevis
COMMUNISM Leslie Holmes
COMPARATIVE LITERATURE
    Ben Hutchinson
COMPLEXITY John H. Holland
THE COMPUTER Darrel Ince
COMPUTER SCIENCE
    Subrata Dasgupta
CONCENTRATION CAMPS
    Dan Stone
CONFUCIANISM Daniel K. Gardner
THE CONQUISTADORS Matthew
    Restall and Felipe Fernández-Armesto
CONSCIENCE Paul Strohm
CONSCIOUSNESS Susan Blackmore
CONTEMPORARY ART
    Julian Stallabrass
CONTEMPORARY FICTION
    Robert Eaglestone
CONTINENTAL PHILOSOPHY
    Simon Critchley
COPERNICUS Owen Gingerich
CORAL REEFS Charles Sheppard
CORPORATE SOCIAL
    RESPONSIBILITY Jeremy Moon
CORRUPTION Leslie Holmes
COSMOLOGY Peter Coles
COUNTRY MUSIC Richard Carlin
CRIME FICTION Richard Bradford
CRIMINAL JUSTICE Julian V. Roberts
CRIMINOLOGY Tim Newburn
CRITICAL THEORY
    Stephen Eric Bronner
THE CRUSADES Christopher Tyerman
CRYPTOGRAPHY Fred Piper and
    Sean Murphy
CRYSTALLOGRAPHY A. M. Glazer
THE CULTURAL REVOLUTION
    Richard Curt Kraus

DADA AND SURREALISM
    David Hopkins
DANTE Peter Hainsworth and
    David Robey
DARWIN Jonathan Howard
THE DEAD SEA SCROLLS
    Timothy H. Lim
DECADENCE David Weir
DECOLONIZATION Dane Kennedy
DEMENTIA Kathleen Taylor
DEMOCRACY Bernard Crick
DEMOGRAPHY Sarah Harper
DEPRESSION Jan Scott and
    Mary Jane Tacchi
DERRIDA Simon Glendinning
DESCARTES Tom Sorell
DESERTS Nick Middleton
DESIGN John Heskett
DEVELOPMENT Ian Goldin
DEVELOPMENTAL BIOLOGY
    Lewis Wolpert
THE DEVIL Darren Oldridge
DIASPORA Kevin Kenny
DICTIONARIES Lynda Mugglestone
DINOSAURS David Norman
DIPLOMACY Joseph M. Siracusa
DOCUMENTARY FILM
    Patricia Aufderheide
DREAMING J. Allan Hobson
DRUGS Les Iversen
DRUIDS Barry Cunliffe
DYNASTY Jeroen Duindam
DYSLEXIA Margaret J. Snowling
EARLY MUSIC Thomas Forrest Kelly
THE EARTH Martin Redfern
EARTH SYSTEM SCIENCE Tim Lenton
ECONOMICS Partha Dasgupta
EDUCATION Gary Thomas
EGYPTIAN MYTH Geraldine Pinch
EIGHTEENTH-CENTURY BRITAIN
    Paul Langford
THE ELEMENTS Philip Ball
ÉMILE ZOLA Brian Nelson
EMOTION Dylan Evans
EMPIRE Stephen Howe
ENERGY SYSTEMS Nick Jenkins
ENGELS Terrell Carver
ENGINEERING David Blockley
THE ENGLISH LANGUAGE
    Simon Horobin
ENGLISH LITERATURE Jonathan Bate

THE ENLIGHTENMENT
John Robertson
ENTREPRENEURSHIP
Paul Westhead and Mike Wright
ENVIRONMENTAL ECONOMICS
Stephen Smith
ENVIRONMENTAL ETHICS
Robin Attfield
ENVIRONMENTAL LAW
Elizabeth Fisher
ENVIRONMENTAL
POLITICS Andrew Dobson
EPICUREANISM Catherine Wilson
EPIDEMIOLOGY Rodolfo Saracci
ETHICS Simon Blackburn
ETHNOMUSICOLOGY Timothy Rice
THE ETRUSCANS Christopher Smith
EUGENICS Philippa Levine
THE EUROPEAN UNION
Simon Usherwood and John Pinder
EUROPEAN UNION LAW
Anthony Arnull
EVOLUTION Brian and
Deborah Charlesworth
EXISTENTIALISM Thomas Flynn
EXPLORATION Stewart A. Weaver
EXTINCTION Paul B. Wignall
THE EYE Michael Land
FAIRY TALE Marina Warner
FAMILY LAW Jonathan Herring
FASCISM Kevin Passmore
FASHION Rebecca Arnold
FEDERALISM Mark J. Rozell and
Clyde Wilcox
FEMINISM Margaret Walters
FILM Michael Wood
FILM MUSIC Kathryn Kalinak
FILM NOIR James Naremore
FIRE Andrew C. Scott
THE FIRST WORLD WAR
Michael Howard
FOLK MUSIC Mark Slobin
FOOD John Krebs
FORENSIC PSYCHOLOGY
David Canter
FORENSIC SCIENCE Jim Fraser
FORESTS Jaboury Ghazoul
FOSSILS Keith Thomson
FOUCAULT Gary Gutting
THE FOUNDING FATHERS
R. B. Bernstein

FRACTALS Kenneth Falconer
FREE SPEECH Nigel Warburton
FREE WILL Thomas Pink
FREEMASONRY Andreas Önnerfors
FRENCH LITERATURE John D. Lyons
FRENCH PHILOSOPHY
Stephen Gaukroger and Knox Peden
THE FRENCH REVOLUTION
William Doyle
FREUD Anthony Storr
FUNDAMENTALISM Malise Ruthven
FUNGI Nicholas P. Money
THE FUTURE Jennifer M. Gidley
GALAXIES John Gribbin
GALILEO Stillman Drake
GAME THEORY Ken Binmore
GANDHI Bhikhu Parekh
GARDEN HISTORY Gordon Campbell
GENES Jonathan Slack
GENIUS Andrew Robinson
GENOMICS John Archibald
GEOFFREY CHAUCER David Wallace
GEOGRAPHY John Matthews and
David Herbert
GEOLOGY Jan Zalasiewicz
GEOPHYSICS William Lowrie
GEOPOLITICS Klaus Dodds
GERMAN LITERATURE Nicholas Boyle
GERMAN PHILOSOPHY
Andrew Bowie
THE GHETTO Bryan Cheyette
GLACIATION David J. A. Evans
GLOBAL CATASTROPHES Bill McGuire
GLOBAL ECONOMIC HISTORY
Robert C. Allen
GLOBALIZATION Manfred Steger
GOD John Bowker
GOETHE Ritchie Robertson
THE GOTHIC Nick Groom
GOVERNANCE Mark Bevir
GRAVITY Timothy Clifton
THE GREAT DEPRESSION AND
THE NEW DEAL Eric Rauchway
HABERMAS James Gordon Finlayson
THE HABSBURG EMPIRE Martyn Rady
HAPPINESS Daniel M. Haybron
THE HARLEM RENAISSANCE
Cheryl A. Wall
THE HEBREW BIBLE AS LITERATURE
Tod Linafelt
HEGEL Peter Singer

HEIDEGGER Michael Inwood
THE HELLENISTIC AGE
    Peter Thonemann
HEREDITY John Waller
HERMENEUTICS Jens Zimmermann
HERODOTUS Jennifer T. Roberts
HIEROGLYPHS Penelope Wilson
HINDUISM Kim Knott
HISTORY John H. Arnold
THE HISTORY OF ASTRONOMY
    Michael Hoskin
THE HISTORY OF CHEMISTRY
    William H. Brock
THE HISTORY OF CHILDHOOD
    James Marten
THE HISTORY OF CINEMA
    Geoffrey Nowell-Smith
THE HISTORY OF LIFE
    Michael Benton
THE HISTORY OF MATHEMATICS
    Jacqueline Stedall
THE HISTORY OF MEDICINE
    William Bynum
THE HISTORY OF PHYSICS
    J. L. Heilbron
THE HISTORY OF TIME
    Leofranc Holford-Strevens
HIV AND AIDS Alan Whiteside
HOBBES Richard Tuck
HOLLYWOOD Peter Decherney
THE HOLY ROMAN EMPIRE
    Joachim Whaley
HOME Michael Allen Fox
HOMER Barbara Graziosi
HORMONES Martin Luck
HUMAN ANATOMY
    Leslie Klenerman
HUMAN EVOLUTION Bernard Wood
HUMAN RIGHTS Andrew Clapham
HUMANISM Stephen Law
HUME A. J. Ayer
HUMOUR Noël Carroll
THE ICE AGE Jamie Woodward
IDENTITY Florian Coulmas
IDEOLOGY Michael Freeden
THE IMMUNE SYSTEM
    Paul Klenerman
INDIAN CINEMA
    Ashish Rajadhyaksha
INDIAN PHILOSOPHY Sue Hamilton

THE INDUSTRIAL REVOLUTION
    Robert C. Allen
INFECTIOUS DISEASE Marta L. Wayne
    and Benjamin M. Bolker
INFINITY Ian Stewart
INFORMATION Luciano Floridi
INNOVATION Mark Dodgson and
    David Gann
INTELLECTUAL PROPERTY
    Siva Vaidhyanathan
INTELLIGENCE Ian J. Deary
INTERNATIONAL LAW Vaughan Lowe
INTERNATIONAL MIGRATION
    Khalid Koser
INTERNATIONAL RELATIONS
    Christian Reus-Smit
INTERNATIONAL SECURITY
    Christopher S. Browning
IRAN Ali M. Ansari
ISLAM Malise Ruthven
ISLAMIC HISTORY Adam Silverstein
ISOTOPES Rob Ellam
ITALIAN LITERATURE
    Peter Hainsworth and David Robey
JESUS Richard Bauckham
JEWISH HISTORY David N. Myers
JOURNALISM Ian Hargreaves
JUDAISM Norman Solomon
JUNG Anthony Stevens
KABBALAH Joseph Dan
KAFKA Ritchie Robertson
KANT Roger Scruton
KEYNES Robert Skidelsky
KIERKEGAARD Patrick Gardiner
KNOWLEDGE Jennifer Nagel
THE KORAN Michael Cook
KOREA Michael J. Seth
LAKES Warwick F. Vincent
LANDSCAPE ARCHITECTURE
    Ian H. Thompson
LANDSCAPES AND
    GEOMORPHOLOGY
    Andrew Goudie and Heather Viles
LANGUAGES Stephen R. Anderson
LATE ANTIQUITY Gillian Clark
LAW Raymond Wacks
THE LAWS OF THERMODYNAMICS
    Peter Atkins
LEADERSHIP Keith Grint
LEARNING Mark Haselgrove

LEIBNIZ Maria Rosa Antognazza
LEO TOLSTOY Liza Knapp
LIBERALISM Michael Freeden
LIGHT Ian Walmsley
LINCOLN Allen C. Guelzo
LINGUISTICS Peter Matthews
LITERARY THEORY Jonathan Culler
LOCKE John Dunn
LOGIC Graham Priest
LOVE Ronald de Sousa
MACHIAVELLI Quentin Skinner
MADNESS Andrew Scull
MAGIC Owen Davies
MAGNA CARTA Nicholas Vincent
MAGNETISM Stephen Blundell
MALTHUS Donald Winch
MAMMALS T. S. Kemp
MANAGEMENT John Hendry
MAO Delia Davin
MARINE BIOLOGY Philip V. Mladenov
THE MARQUIS DE SADE John Phillips
MARTIN LUTHER Scott H. Hendrix
MARTYRDOM Jolyon Mitchell
MARX Peter Singer
MATERIALS Christopher Hall
MATHEMATICAL FINANCE
    Mark H. A. Davis
MATHEMATICS Timothy Gowers
MATTER Geoff Cottrell
THE MEANING OF LIFE Terry Eagleton
MEASUREMENT David Hand
MEDICAL ETHICS Michael Dunn and
    Tony Hope
MEDICAL LAW Charles Foster
MEDIEVAL BRITAIN John Gillingham
    and Ralph A. Griffiths
MEDIEVAL LITERATURE
    Elaine Treharne
MEDIEVAL PHILOSOPHY
    John Marenbon
MEMORY Jonathan K. Foster
METAPHYSICS Stephen Mumford
METHODISM William J. Abraham
THE MEXICAN REVOLUTION
    Alan Knight
MICHAEL FARADAY
    Frank A. J. L. James
MICROBIOLOGY Nicholas P. Money
MICROECONOMICS Avinash Dixit
MICROSCOPY Terence Allen

THE MIDDLE AGES Miri Rubin
MILITARY JUSTICE Eugene R. Fidell
MILITARY STRATEGY
    Antulio J. Echevarria II
MINERALS David Vaughan
MIRACLES Yujin Nagasawa
MODERN ARCHITECTURE
    Adam Sharr
MODERN ART David Cottington
MODERN CHINA Rana Mitter
MODERN DRAMA
    Kirsten E. Shepherd-Barr
MODERN FRANCE
    Vanessa R. Schwartz
MODERN INDIA Craig Jeffrey
MODERN IRELAND Senia Pašeta
MODERN ITALY Anna Cento Bull
MODERN JAPAN
    Christopher Goto-Jones
MODERN LATIN AMERICAN
    LITERATURE
    Roberto González Echevarría
MODERN WAR Richard English
MODERNISM Christopher Butler
MOLECULAR BIOLOGY Aysha Divan
    and Janice A. Royds
MOLECULES Philip Ball
MONASTICISM Stephen J. Davis
THE MONGOLS Morris Rossabi
MOONS David A. Rothery
MORMONISM Richard Lyman Bushman
MOUNTAINS Martin F. Price
MUHAMMAD Jonathan A. C. Brown
MULTICULTURALISM Ali Rattansi
MULTILINGUALISM John C. Maher
MUSIC Nicholas Cook
MYTH Robert A. Segal
NAPOLEON David Bell
THE NAPOLEONIC WARS
    Mike Rapport
NATIONALISM Steven Grosby
NATIVE AMERICAN LITERATURE
    Sean Teuton
NAVIGATION Jim Bennett
NAZI GERMANY Jane Caplan
NELSON MANDELA Elleke Boehmer
NEOLIBERALISM Manfred Steger and
    Ravi Roy
NETWORKS Guido Caldarelli and
    Michele Catanzaro

THE NEW TESTAMENT
    Luke Timothy Johnson
THE NEW TESTAMENT AS
    LITERATURE Kyle Keefer
NEWTON Robert Iliffe
NIELS BOHR J. L. Heilbron
NIETZSCHE Michael Tanner
NINETEENTH-CENTURY BRITAIN
    Christopher Harvie and
    H. C. G. Matthew
THE NORMAN CONQUEST
    George Garnett
NORTH AMERICAN
    INDIANS Theda Perdue and
    Michael D. Green
NORTHERN IRELAND
    Marc Mulholland
NOTHING Frank Close
NUCLEAR PHYSICS Frank Close
NUCLEAR POWER Maxwell Irvine
NUCLEAR WEAPONS
    Joseph M. Siracusa
NUMBER THEORY Robin Wilson
NUMBERS Peter M. Higgins
NUTRITION David A. Bender
OBJECTIVITY Stephen Gaukroger
OCEANS Dorrik Stow
THE OLD TESTAMENT
    Michael D. Coogan
THE ORCHESTRA D. Kern Holoman
ORGANIC CHEMISTRY
    Graham Patrick
ORGANIZATIONS Mary Jo Hatch
ORGANIZED CRIME
    Georgios A. Antonopoulos and
    Georgios Papanicolaou
ORTHODOX CHRISTIANITY
    A. Edward Siecienski
PAGANISM Owen Davies
PAIN Rob Boddice
THE PALESTINIAN-ISRAELI
    CONFLICT Martin Bunton
PANDEMICS Christian W. McMillen
PARTICLE PHYSICS Frank Close
PAUL E. P. Sanders
PEACE Oliver P. Richmond
PENTECOSTALISM William K. Kay
PERCEPTION Brian Rogers
THE PERIODIC TABLE Eric R. Scerri
PHILOSOPHY Edward Craig

PHILOSOPHY IN THE ISLAMIC
    WORLD Peter Adamson
PHILOSOPHY OF BIOLOGY
    Samir Okasha
PHILOSOPHY OF LAW
    Raymond Wacks
PHILOSOPHY OF SCIENCE
    Samir Okasha
PHILOSOPHY OF RELIGION
    Tim Bayne
PHOTOGRAPHY Steve Edwards
PHYSICAL CHEMISTRY Peter Atkins
PHYSICS Sidney Perkowitz
PILGRIMAGE Ian Reader
PLAGUE Paul Slack
PLANETS David A. Rothery
PLANTS Timothy Walker
PLATE TECTONICS Peter Molnar
PLATO Julia Annas
POETRY Bernard O'Donoghue
POLITICAL PHILOSOPHY David Miller
POLITICS Kenneth Minogue
POPULISM Cas Mudde and
    Cristóbal Rovira Kaltwasser
POSTCOLONIALISM Robert Young
POSTMODERNISM Christopher Butler
POSTSTRUCTURALISM
    Catherine Belsey
POVERTY Philip N. Jefferson
PREHISTORY Chris Gosden
PRESOCRATIC PHILOSOPHY
    Catherine Osborne
PRIVACY Raymond Wacks
PROBABILITY John Haigh
PROGRESSIVISM Walter Nugent
PROHIBITION W. J. Rorabaugh
PROJECTS Andrew Davies
PROTESTANTISM Mark A. Noll
PSYCHIATRY Tom Burns
PSYCHOANALYSIS Daniel Pick
PSYCHOLOGY Gillian Butler and
    Freda McManus
PSYCHOLOGY OF MUSIC
    Elizabeth Hellmuth Margulis
PSYCHOPATHY Essi Viding
PSYCHOTHERAPY Tom Burns and
    Eva Burns-Lundgren
PUBLIC ADMINISTRATION
    Stella Z. Theodoulou and Ravi K. Roy
PUBLIC HEALTH Virginia Berridge

PURITANISM Francis J. Bremer
THE QUAKERS Pink Dandelion
QUANTUM THEORY
   John Polkinghorne
RACISM Ali Rattansi
RADIOACTIVITY Claudio Tuniz
RASTAFARI Ennis B. Edmonds
READING Belinda Jack
THE REAGAN REVOLUTION Gil Troy
REALITY Jan Westerhoff
RECONSTRUCTION Allen C. Guelzo
THE REFORMATION Peter Marshall
RELATIVITY Russell Stannard
RELIGION IN AMERICA Timothy Beal
THE RENAISSANCE Jerry Brotton
RENAISSANCE ART
   Geraldine A. Johnson
RENEWABLE ENERGY Nick Jelley
REPTILES T. S. Kemp
REVOLUTIONS Jack A. Goldstone
RHETORIC Richard Toye
RISK Baruch Fischhoff and John Kadvany
RITUAL Barry Stephenson
RIVERS Nick Middleton
ROBOTICS Alan Winfield
ROCKS Jan Zalasiewicz
ROMAN BRITAIN Peter Salway
THE ROMAN EMPIRE
   Christopher Kelly
THE ROMAN REPUBLIC
   David M. Gwynn
ROMANTICISM Michael Ferber
ROUSSEAU Robert Wokler
RUSSELL A. C. Grayling
THE RUSSIAN ECONOMY
   Richard Connolly
RUSSIAN HISTORY Geoffrey Hosking
RUSSIAN LITERATURE Catriona Kelly
THE RUSSIAN
   REVOLUTION S. A. Smith
THE SAINTS Simon Yarrow
SAVANNAS Peter A. Furley
SCEPTICISM Duncan Pritchard
SCHIZOPHRENIA Chris Frith and
   Eve Johnstone
SCHOPENHAUER
   Christopher Janaway
SCIENCE AND RELIGION
   Thomas Dixon
SCIENCE FICTION David Seed

THE SCIENTIFIC REVOLUTION
   Lawrence M. Principe
SCOTLAND Rab Houston
SECULARISM Andrew Copson
SEXUAL SELECTION Marlene Zuk and
   Leigh W. Simmons
SEXUALITY Véronique Mottier
SHAKESPEARE'S COMEDIES
   Bart van Es
SHAKESPEARE'S SONNETS AND
   POEMS Jonathan F. S. Post
SHAKESPEARE'S TRAGEDIES
   Stanley Wells
SIKHISM Eleanor Nesbitt
THE SILK ROAD James A. Millward
SLANG Jonathon Green
SLEEP Steven W. Lockley and
   Russell G. Foster
SMELL Matthew Cobb
SOCIAL AND CULTURAL
   ANTHROPOLOGY
   John Monaghan and Peter Just
SOCIAL PSYCHOLOGY Richard J. Crisp
SOCIAL WORK Sally Holland and
   Jonathan Scourfield
SOCIALISM Michael Newman
SOCIOLINGUISTICS John Edwards
SOCIOLOGY Steve Bruce
SOCRATES C. C. W. Taylor
SOUND Mike Goldsmith
SOUTHEAST ASIA James R. Rush
THE SOVIET UNION Stephen Lovell
THE SPANISH CIVIL WAR
   Helen Graham
SPANISH LITERATURE Jo Labanyi
SPINOZA Roger Scruton
SPIRITUALITY Philip Sheldrake
SPORT Mike Cronin
STARS Andrew King
STATISTICS David J. Hand
STEM CELLS Jonathan Slack
STOICISM Brad Inwood
STRUCTURAL ENGINEERING
   David Blockley
STUART BRITAIN John Morrill
THE SUN Philip Judge
SUPERCONDUCTIVITY
   Stephen Blundell
SUPERSTITION Stuart Vyse
SYMMETRY Ian Stewart

SYNAESTHESIA Julia Simner
SYNTHETIC BIOLOGY Jamie A. Davies
SYSTEMS BIOLOGY Eberhard O. Voit
TAXATION Stephen Smith
TEETH Peter S. Ungar
TELESCOPES Geoff Cottrell
TERRORISM Charles Townshend
THEATRE Marvin Carlson
THEOLOGY David F. Ford
THINKING AND REASONING
    Jonathan St B. T. Evans
THOMAS AQUINAS Fergus Kerr
THOUGHT Tim Bayne
TIBETAN BUDDHISM
    Matthew T. Kapstein
TIDES David George Bowers and
    Emyr Martyn Roberts
TOCQUEVILLE Harvey C. Mansfield
TOPOLOGY Richard Earl
TRAGEDY Adrian Poole
TRANSLATION Matthew Reynolds
THE TREATY OF VERSAILLES
    Michael S. Neiberg
TRIGONOMETRY
    Glen Van Brummelen
THE TROJAN WAR
    Eric H. Cline
TRUST Katherine Hawley
THE TUDORS John Guy
TWENTIETH-CENTURY
    BRITAIN Kenneth O. Morgan
TYPOGRAPHY Paul Luna
THE UNITED NATIONS
    Jussi M. Hanhimäki

UNIVERSITIES AND COLLEGES
    David Palfreyman and Paul Temple
THE U.S. CIVIL WAR Louis P. Masur
THE U.S. CONGRESS Donald A. Ritchie
THE U.S. CONSTITUTION
    David J. Bodenhamer
THE U.S. SUPREME COURT
    Linda Greenhouse
UTILITARIANISM
    Katarzyna de Lazari-Radek and
    Peter Singer
UTOPIANISM Lyman Tower Sargent
VETERINARY SCIENCE James Yeates
THE VIKINGS Julian D. Richards
VIRUSES Dorothy H. Crawford
VOLTAIRE Nicholas Cronk
WAR AND TECHNOLOGY
    Alex Roland
WATER John Finney
WAVES Mike Goldsmith
WEATHER Storm Dunlop
THE WELFARE STATE David Garland
WILLIAM SHAKESPEARE
    Stanley Wells
WITCHCRAFT Malcolm Gaskill
WITTGENSTEIN A. C. Grayling
WORK Stephen Fineman
WORLD MUSIC Philip Bohlman
THE WORLD TRADE
    ORGANIZATION Amrita Narlikar
WORLD WAR II Gerhard L. Weinberg
WRITING AND SCRIPT
    Andrew Robinson
ZIONISM Michael Stanislawski

Available soon:

GEORGE BERNARD SHAW
    Christopher Wixson
ECOLOGY Jaboury Ghazoul
MODERN BRAZIL Anthony W. Pereira

SOFT MATTER
    Tom McLeish
PHILOSOPHICAL METHOD
    Timothy Williamson

For more information visit our website

www.oup.com/vsi/

Bryan Cheyette

THE GHETTO

A Very Short Introduction

OXFORD
UNIVERSITY PRESS

OXFORD
UNIVERSITY PRESS

Great Clarendon Street, Oxford, OX2 6DP,
United Kingdom

Oxford University Press is a department of the University of Oxford.
It furthers the University's objective of excellence in research, scholarship,
and education by publishing worldwide. Oxford is a registered trade mark of
Oxford University Press in the UK and in certain other countries

© Bryan Cheyette 2020

The moral rights of the author have been asserted

First edition published in 2020

Impression: 1

Published in the United States of America by Oxford University Press
198 Madison Avenue, New York, NY 10016, United States of America

British Library Cataloguing in Publication Data
Data available

Library of Congress Control Number: 2020936023

ISBN 978-0-19-880995-1

Printed in Great Britain by
Ashford Colour Press Ltd, Gosport, Hampshire

Links to third party websites are provided by Oxford in good faith and
for information only. Oxford disclaims any responsibility for the materials
contained in any third party website referenced in this work.

To Sonia Cheyette (1932–2018)

Contents

Acknowledgements xvii

List of illustrations xxi

1 Why ghetto? 1

2 The Age of the Ghetto 14

3 Ghettos of the imagination 39

4 Nazism and the ghetto 61

5 The ghetto in America 88

6 The global ghetto 118

References 127

Further reading 135

Index 139

Acknowledgements

Writing this book has been great fun and has challenged the limits of my understanding at every turn. Along with the research facilities at the University of Reading, I am grateful to many individuals and institutions that enabled me to complete this study. Early ideas on the topic were expedited by a 2017 conference on the history of the ghetto co-organized by the Pears Institute at Birkbeck College, London, and my university. The Department of English Literature at Reading, in the guise of David Brauner, Michelle O'Callaghan, Steven Matthews, Peter Stoneley, and Gail Marshall, was characteristically generous and funded the appointment of Emma Cowley as an exemplary research assistant. The 2017 conference gave me a chance to hear the latest thinking on the topic from Shaul Bassi, Mitchell Duneier, Emily Michelson, Dan Michman, and Filippo De Vivo. David Feldman, Director of the Pears Institute, and Brendan McGeever, Deputy Director, have both been essential interlocutors and Jan Davidson made sure that the conference worked effectively.

At other Pears Institute events I have been fortunate enough to hear Bernard Dov Cooperman speak, who is an important influence, and to hear new research on London's East End ghetto from Nadia Valman. Research trips to Venice, thanks to Shaul

Bassi, and to Rome, thanks to Emily Michelson, enabled my ideas to become concrete in more ways than one.

The Special Collections at the University of Southampton, part of the Parkes Institute, has been an essential resource for rare and unusual books on the ghetto. With his usual kindness, Tony Kushner, the founding director of the institute, not only renewed my fellowship but also invited me to give a keynote on the topic. Other keynotes have been delivered at the University of Durham, thanks to Yulia Egorova; Manchester Metropolitan University, thanks to Andrew Crome; Warwick University, thanks to Rebekah Vince; King's College, London, thanks to Andrea Schatz; and Cambridge University, thanks to Simon Goldhill. Susannah Heschel, the most big-hearted of colleagues, invited me to speak on the African-American ghetto at Dartmouth College to celebrate the twenty-fifth anniversary of Cornel West's *Race Matters* (1993).

Robert Eaglestone and Steve Zipperstein were two early and astute readers of this work and David Ruderman was an invaluable guide. The late David Cesarani has been, and continues to be, a life-long influence not only on the Nazi period but on my understanding of history in general. David and Susie Herman, Miriam and Stephen Grabiner, Dawn Waterman, Haidee Becker, Louise Sylvester and Anthony Metzer, and Alan and Melanie Craig are a source of daily wisdom on this topic and much else. I am especially grateful to the Blue Thread charity for enabling me to buy out some of my teaching. But without the editors at OUP this book would not have been possible. The inestimable Andrea Keegan commissioned it and saw it through until it was half written. Luciana O'Flaherty has been a meticulous reader saving me from many infelicities; and Jenny Nugee has guided the book, with great care, through all stages of production. The anonymous reader has improved the manuscript considerably.

Jacob Cheyette has been an important source of information on Hip Hop and Rap which will continue long after publication. Susan Cooklin, with characteristic love and generosity, has made this and all of my publications possible over more than three decades. My mother, Sonia Cheyette, sadly died when I was working on the book. I dedicate it to her memory.

List of illustrations

1 The Frankfurt *Judengasse* (Jew's alley) **5**
Classic Image / Alamy Stock Photo.

2 Venice Ghetto (contemporary woodcut) **19**
Jacopo de' Barbari, *View of Venice*, 1500. The Cleveland Museum of Art. *The Cleveland Museum of Art Handbook*. Cleveland, OH: The Cleveland Museum of Art, 1958. Mentioned and Reproduced: cat. no. 628, 629 archive.org.

3 Rome ghetto (1555–1870) **25**
FALKENSTEINFOTO / Alamy Stock Photo.

4 *The Volunteer* (1834) by Moritz Daniel Oppenheim **43**
Heritage Image Partnership Ltd / Alamy Stock Photo.

5 New York's Lower East Side **55**

Granger Historical Picture Archive / Alamy Stock Photo.

6 Łódź ghetto workforce **70**
Prisma by Dukas Presseagentur GmbH / Alamy Stock Photo.

7 The destruction of the Warsaw ghetto after the uprising **82**
World History Archive / Alamy Stock Photo.

8 Chicago's second ghetto **101**
PF-(usna) / Alamy Stock Photo.

9 Harlem's Renaissance **108**
Photo by Michael Ochs Archives / Getty Images.

10 Soweto **120**
Blaine Harrington III / Alamy Stock Photo.

11 Urban segregation **122**
David R. Frazier Photolibrary, Inc. / Alamy Stock Photo.

Chapter 1
Why ghetto?

The word 'ghetto' has layers of contradictory meanings accrued over half a millennium and a bewildering array of contexts across much of the world. Most agree that there is neither a single place nor a fixed idea which encompasses 'the ghetto'. As we will see, the history of the ghetto began as a defining aspect of Jewish history in the medieval and early modern period in Western and Central Europe. By the 19th century it was a free-floating concept which travelled to Eastern Europe and the United States. In the mid-20th century, ghettos were crudely rehabilitated by the Nazis in the name of medieval tradition and, yet later, the term was routinely applied to endemic black ghettoization in America. In the 21st century, 'the ghetto' has become ubiquitous—everywhere and nowhere—and has been applied to urban slums, townships, *banlieues*, and *favela* in Europe, Asia, the Middle East, Africa, and Latin America.

The slipperiness of 'ghetto' as both place and concept should not be underestimated. Does it just apply to a particular ethnic or racial group? Is it a term of abuse or resistance? A way of understanding commonplace urbanization or a unique form of racial segregation? Is it a profound indication of how people are divided along class lines in the global metropolis? Or is it merely a superficial aspect of global culture (popular music, fiction, film, and fashion)? Few can decide whether the term is old or new; local or global; ordinary or extreme.

This book aims to answer basic questions about the ghetto—why, when, where, what, and for whom—in order to make sense of this unstable word. The ghetto can be understood only after we trace where particular ghettos were formed, see who lived in them, ask why and when they were created, and know what exactly constituted a ghetto. With this basic but elusive information we can see how different ghettos interrelate, or are contrasted, across five centuries and much of the world. As each chapter will illustrate, such comparisons are complicated as ghettos varied greatly even in the same general environment. 'Ghetto' hardly ever means one thing. Such multiplicity is further confounded when we note that the word 'ghetto', from the beginning, was symbolic as well as descriptive and often resonated far beyond a specific location. Imagined ghettos are, paradoxically, more evocative than actual or historic ghettos. In short, the rich complexity of ghetto phenomena cannot be reduced to a single reality or a single image.

During the Age of the Ghetto (1516–1789), as it is known, it is possible to define ghettos straightforwardly as 'compulsory, segregated, and enclosed' dwellings in the historian Bernard Ravid's standard formulation. This hard definition has, in the modern period, gradually softened so as to include voluntary and open ghettos. But the history of the ghetto does not follow a linear narrative moving from hard to soft definitions. Ghettos include both the softer history of urbanization and class segregation as well as the harder history of racial differentiation. Both histories continue in tandem to this day. It is this instability that has enabled the ghetto— as image and reality; in its hard and softer forms—to endure.

Origins

Before there were ghettos, there were 'Jewish quarters', otherwise known as 'Judengasse', 'Judenstadt', 'Guidecca', 'Juiverie', 'Juderia',

'Judaismo', 'Judaiche'. These were only a few of the names given to the alleys or streets or localities where Jews lived in Christian Europe during the Middle Ages. From the 5th to the 15th centuries Jews resided in roughly permanent and separate areas in parts of Spain and the Italian peninsula, in Germanic and French lands, in Britain and the Low Countries, and in small towns throughout Central and Eastern Europe. Throughout the Ottoman Empire (from the early 1300s to the early 1900s) Jews also wore distinguishing clothing and lived in Jewish quarters. Ottoman rule was much more tolerant than its Christian equivalent. Whereas nations in Western Europe expelled most Jews from the 12th to the 15th centuries, the Ottoman rulers welcomed them.

As Jews were a tiny European minority (less than 3 per cent of the general population), the subject of Jewish residence was raised rarely by the Catholic Church during this period. The Third Lateran Council of 1179 prohibited Christians living in the homes of Jews or acting as servants for Jews; the Fourth Lateran Council of 1215 introduced a compulsory yellow patch for Jews and Muslims. Just over 200 years later, in the Council of Basel (1434), Jews were forbidden to cohabitate with Christians and were told to live far away from churches. At a local level, church councils attempted to segregate Jews on this basis. But ghettos were first formed in the 16th century. They are not part of medieval history.

Understood in relation to Church doctrine, 'perfidious Jewry' was a form of impurity awaiting salvific conversion. Only the conversion of the Jews could bring about the Second Coming of Christ, which is the reason why many medieval popes safeguarded Jewish communities in readiness for the return of the messiah. This was the symbolic function of the secluded Jewish quarter but such quarters were not simply a response to medieval Judeophobia. Jews lived in *Kehillot Kadoshot* (holy communities) voluntarily, to gain protection and out of a sense of religious unity. In secular terms, Jews were *servi camerae* (servants of the Treasury), unlike slaves or peasants, and successive local rulers made them liable for tax payment.

Most sizeable Jewish quarters, such as those in Prague and Frankfurt, were the equivalent of medieval corporations. These were legally recognized communities with distinct rights and duties. They enjoyed internal autonomy and so were self-governed, paid taxes, and had elaborate institutional structures based around the Synagogue. These houses of worship doubled as nascent town halls with civil and criminal cases judged by rabbinical courts. Those who lived communally enjoyed social welfare, health, education, and burial rights in a local cemetery and were cared for from birth until death. Sixteenth-century ghettos followed this pattern.

The Christian majority, in response to economic competition, attacked and expelled local Jews. That is why ruling town councils encouraged Jewish spatial segregation on the grounds of maintaining law and order. They wanted to keep their Jewish servants of the Treasury safe so as to ensure economic activity and the consequent high rates of taxation. Jews concurred, for the most part, on a voluntary basis. These quarters were sometimes walled and gated as populated areas at the time were routinely walled and gated throughout Europe and North Africa. They were most often locked from the inside for self-protection. Medieval Jews could mix socially and trade with the local Christian population as their dwellings tended to be voluntary, porous, and communal.

The *Judengasse*

By the 15th century, most famously in Frankfurt am Main but also in Prague, Jewish quarters became less voluntary, anticipating later ghettos. The Frankfurt *Judengasse* (Jew's alley) was created in 1462 and demolished in 1811 (see Figure 1). It conformed to the hard definition of ghettoization—'compulsory, segregated and enclosed'—and was walled, gated, and under curfew. This contrasted with virtually every other Jewish quarter in the 15th century. Exceptions to this rule were the Juderías and Morerías in

1. The Frankfurt *Judengasse* (Jew's alley).

Spain in 1480 where Jews and Moslems were compelled to live in segregated and enclosed quarters. It was the perceived failure of the policy of segregation—leading to the supposed 'contamination' of Catholic Spain—that led to the expulsion of Jews and Muslims in 1492.

But rather than Catholic Spain, it was the city of Frankfurt and the region of Bohemia (both at the heart of the anti-Catholic Reformation), which anticipated the ghettoization of north-central Catholic Italy. A few hundred Jews, initially, were compelled to live in a narrow lane ('gasse') in Frankfurt which was no more than 4 or 5 yards wide, and around 330 yards long. At first there were fewer than a hundred tenement houses walled together. One side of the curved street backed onto the River Main and only three gates, which were guarded, could be used to exit and enter during daylight hours.

The only comparable 'Jewish quarter' of its size and influence was the *Josefov* (as it was eventually known) in the Old Town of Prague which was created in the 13th century and occupied around 6 acres before 1389. Like Frankfurt, the Jewish quarter of Prague was built close to major European trading routes. In the early years, Christian guilds, as elsewhere in Europe, organized regular attacks and expulsions (once killing 1,500 residents) from the Jewish quarter. But, as with Frankfurt, local sovereigns valued the high taxes (or 'special contributions') from Prague Jews and the trading networks which wealthier Jews could open up. The Jewish quarter in the Old Town of Prague eventually became a self-governing medieval corporation with a rich Jewish and Bohemian cultural life.

The *Judengasse*, which was about half the size of its Bohemian equivalent, eventually expanded to approximately three thousand inhabitants over nearly three centuries. This made it one of the most overcrowded districts in Europe. Around 190 tenement houses had floors added to them with rooms split or shared between several families. Over the decades, houses were added front and back, including in the city's moat, which were four tenements deep. Flat rooftops also provided new dwellings. But fire was a constant risk and the street was badly damaged in 1711 and 1721 (where it was rebuilt in a more modern form) and in 1796 by Napoleon's army (which in effect ended the district).

The Frankfurt *Judengasse* anticipated both the precarious building-work in compulsory 'ghetto' enclosures and the more general policy of ghettoization on the Italian peninsula. On a smaller scale, Worms and Würzburg in the German lands prefigured the Italian model by segregating rather than expelling its Jewish residents. Every other German state and nearly all of Western Europe expelled their Jews until the 17th century. The Frankfurt *Judengasse* was a compromise in Western Europe as it reinforced a policy of segregation rather than expulsion. But the overcrowded and heavily taxed population of the 'Jew's alley', forced to wear yellow patches, did not feel like they had been granted a concession. Its residents described their narrow lane as a 'new Egypt'. The nearby Dominican Monastery organized regular attacks on the *Judengasse* which occasionally resulted in it being overrun completely. No wonder its occupants compared themselves to the Israelite slaves of Egypt.

A good deal of pressure was placed on the ruling authorities, mainly from competing economic guilds, to expel the Jews of Frankfurt. But its rulers (eventually overseen by the Holy Roman Emperor) resisted expulsion on pragmatic grounds. The *Judengasse* was an important component in making the Free Imperial City of Frankfurt a major European trading centre. That is why it lasted so long. Meyer Amschel Rothschild was born and raised in its tenements in 1744 where he founded the Rothschild banking dynasty. Silk, grain, cloth, and wine were particularly traded in the *Judengasse*. Along with trade, it also became an important European centre of Jewish spiritually publishing influential books on Kabbalah (mysticism) and Talmud (law).

Following the autonomous structure of medieval Jewish quarters, the Synagogue (known as the *Altschul*) took centre stage in collecting taxes and providing welfare and education to its mainly impoverished inhabitants.

The Janus-faced nature of ghettoization encompassed medieval Judeophobia, on the one hand, and the Rothschild banking dynasty, on the other. This made an understanding of ghettos increasingly unstable. In the medieval period Jewish quarters were created in populated areas and had a crucial commercial as well as a religious function. They were as much an aspect of forward-looking merchant trading as well as backward-looking Catholic theology. The *Judengasse* illustrated this doubleness—symbolizing both the impurity of Jews and their economic usefulness—before this pragmatic ambiguity was writ large in Italy. By the end of the 18th century, twenty-four Italian ghettos had been created over a 300-year period. Some were destitute and impoverished; others were mercantile power-houses; and all contributed greatly to Jewish religious and secular culture. But no two ghettos were the same.

Birth of a word

The Frankfurt *Judengasse* and Prague *Josefov* were not called ghettos during their lifetimes as this would have been anachronistic. The word 'ghetto' did not apply to compulsory, enclosed, and segregated Jewish quarters until 1516. Ghetto or *geto* derived from the Venetian dialect and originated from the verb *getar* 'to pour' (as in molten copper). It referred initially to a municipal copper foundry on the northern outskirts of Venice known as the Ghetto Nuovo. This is the short answer to *when* ghettos (*qua* ghettos) were formed. In 1516, around 500 Jewish men, women, and children, refugees in Venice, were compelled to live on the island under curfew. This was both a product of realpolitik—the inclusion of Jewish bankers into the Venetian economy—as well as of fierce Catholic sermonizing against

Jewish refugees who, for centuries, had been prohibited from living in Venice.

But this most incendiary of words had an inauspicious beginning. It was not until 1571 that 'ghetto' (which, after all, merely referred to an obscure Venetian island) was used officially to denote the founding of the Florentine ghetto. In 1589, the *Seraglio degli Hebrei* (or the 'enclosure of the Jews') became officially known as a 'ghetto' thirty-four years after it was formed in Rome. Italian dialects varied considerably and it took decades before the Venetian 'ghetto' travelled first of all to Florence and then to Rome. In the meantime, Roman Jews preferred the alternative 'ghet' (the Hebrew for 'bill of divorce') to express what it meant for the oldest of diaspora communities, integrated into Rome for millennia, to live separately. The Hebrew 'ghet', at the end of the 16th century, was soon amalgamated with the Venetian 'ghetto'.

The Ghetto Nuovissimo was founded in Venice in 1633 adjacent to the original island foundry. With this act, the word 'ghetto' changed from a noun, indicating a specific district, to an adjective describing a place in general where Jews were forced to live. By the 17th century, ghetto was used with increased frequency in official Italian documents. It was no longer just associated with an unknown island in Venice. Although it became a widespread descriptive term in Italian, it was not used in the German language to any extent until the 19th century. The word 'ghetto' was popularized in French a few decades later and in English in the 1890s. By the 20th century, ghetto resonated globally.

Imagined ghettos

Ghettos from the beginning were imagined in a range of distinct ways well beyond their particular circumstance. One answer to where ghettos were located is in the popular imagination. If Catholics thought of the ghetto as a place of spiritual debasement, Jews, also using a religious mindset, thought of ghettos as holy communities. That is why ghettos were often imagined as a sacred place or a 'New Jerusalem'. From the 16th to the 18th centuries, ghettoized Jews in Italy resisted concerted Catholic efforts to convert them, and even drew on abstruse Kabbalistic traditions and messianic mysticism to turn the ghetto into a spiritual fortress.

The 'Jew's city', as many large-sized Italian ghettos (with a few thousand occupants) were known, were run in a modern manner as small towns. The corporate structure remained from medieval times and included welfare provision, commercial shopping areas, and religious and secular education for men and often women. But no one thought of ghettos at the time as a gateway into the modern world. Today it is possible to associate Italian ghettos with tax-collecting, state planning, urban-zoning, mercantile economics, professionalization, women's agency, a rich cultural life, and legal regulation.

Napoleon Bonaparte's revolutionary army liberated all Italian ghettos (apart from Rome) in 1797. As they demolished the large wooden gates of the ghettos, Bonaparte's soldiers read out an official decree: 'remove that mark of separation between the Jewish Citizens and the other Citizens where no mark should exist'. Some ghettos were renamed, for a short while, 'Neighbourhoods of Reunion' with 'Trees of Liberty' planted ceremoniously in a *piazza* or square. This was the predominant narrative following the French Revolution. Ghettos were the opposite of modernity. Two decades after Western European ghettos were closed, the imagined ghetto symbolized the counter-narrative to the modern nation-state. They were 'backward', 'medieval', and 'regressive', and were associated irretrievably with a barbaric past.

Up until the 1870s, as Jews strived for equal rights throughout Western Europe, the ghetto was perceived as an impediment to modern citizenship. The imagined ghetto moved irrevocably eastwards at least in the German language and replaced the

Yiddish name for a rural Jewish township—*shtetl* or *shtetlach*—in Eastern Europe. From the 1840s to the 1870s, a large number of popular ghetto novels in Germany relocated a free-floating ghetto to rural east-central Europe. A related form of artistic and cultural nostalgia associated a range of Jewish religious practice with the spiritual richness of the ghetto. But such nostalgia, however overtly sympathetic, reinforced perceptions of the ghetto as blinkered and inward looking when compared to the freedom and openness of emancipation.

Ghetto as a travelling concept

As we will see, by the end of the 19th century, the concept of the ghetto travelled west, across the Atlantic, to the United States. Over 250,000 German-Jews immigrated to the United States from the 1820s to the 1920s and brought with them a profound dislike of the ghetto. The concept was popularized in the 1890s with the publication of Israel Zangwill's transatlantic bestseller *Children of the Ghetto: A Study of a Peculiar People* (1892) which was turned into a hit Broadway play. Ghettos were associated with the living conditions of newly arrived Eastern European Jews into Western Europe and the United States. Following Zangwill, dozens of American writers produced lasting ghetto fiction in the early decades of the 20th century.

Unlike the European tradition of ghetto fiction, this later group of writers focused on contemporary urban enclaves of East European immigrants throughout the main cities of Britain and America. While 19th-century German writers placed the ghetto firmly in the rural past, by the 20th century, the ghetto was associated with the present-day urban landscape of most major Western cities. This transformed the free-floating ghetto as it moved in the 19th century from past to present, rural to urban, medieval to modern.

Throughout the 19th century, the imaginary ghetto turned into a travelling concept which changed its meaning as it crossed continents. German-Jewish immigrants brought to the United States an account of the 'medieval' ghetto which contradicted their dream of assimilating fully into their new homeland. For them the ghetto (including the modern urban ghetto) clashed with their enlightened ideal of becoming good emancipated citizens.

By the 20th century, the idea of the ghetto had travelled throughout Europe and the United States, and was impossible to pin down. Was it real or imagined? Was it located in the present or the past? Did it refer to a place or a state of mind? But, with the rise of Nazism, the ghetto was once again fixed in time and space, and was understood overwhelmingly as a form of brutal imprisonment for a supposedly inferior 'race'. The many hundreds of East European ghettos constructed during World War II reinforced the Nazi image of East European Jews (*Ostjuden*) as transmitters of disease locally and of a degenerate 'Jewish spirit' globally. Jews, who resisted their cruel circumstances as much as possible, were deemed a threat by the Nazis that needed containing.

From the 1940s to the 1960s, the history of Nazi ghettoization was applied to the racial 'segregation' of black Americans confined to poor black neighbourhoods in America's major northern cities since the 1920s. In the decades after the war, African-American neighbourhoods were universally discriminated against and associated increasingly with the extremes of European ghettoization. African-Americans, as I will argue, were the only ethno-racial group in the United States where the ghetto was not a staging post on the way to modernity but, instead, a prevalent form of confinement and control which has lasted for a century and still continues. This version of ghettoization has, in the second half of the 20th century, located the idea and place of the ghetto firmly in the United States.

By the time African-Americans took up the idea of 'ghetto' to represent their own severe discrimination it could travel in several directions at once. Some African-Americans referred back to the original early modern ghettos in Italy, others looked to the ethnic enclaves at the turn of the century which were imagined as 'ghettos', and others still looked to the barbarity of Nazi ghettoization. These historical analogies, as the sociologist Mitchell Duneier has argued, reflect different aspects of impoverished black neighbourhoods.

The African-American version of ghettoization has been exported throughout the world as film, fashion, music, and literature. Given its impact on global culture, it is now difficult to think of the ghetto in any other way. But there is an enormous gulf, once again, between image and reality. The Nazi policy of ghettoization was a form of genocidal racial differentiation which was taken up by many African-Americans campaigning for civil rights. Today the ghetto is closely associated with African-American identity just as it was once associated with Jewish identity. But, as we will see, it remains a heavily contested term lauded by some; treated as taboo by others.

Chapter 2
The Age of the Ghetto

The Age of the Ghetto, as it is commonly called, originated
in Italy in the mid-16th century and concluded with the French
Revolution at the end of the 18th century. During this period,
twenty-four ghettos of approximately 30,000 inhabitants were
created in northern and central Italy and became part of the
urban landscape. The Italian peninsula was made up of
belligerent city-states and was ruled by princes and noblemen who
had competing mercantile empires and currencies and spoke in
radically different dialects. Each city-state varied significantly in
relation to papal authority and their attitude to foreign traders.
With such divisions, the policy of ghettoization was far from
uniform. While Venice inaugurated the Italian ghetto in 1516, and
introduced the nomenclature into Western European culture, the
last ghetto was not formed until 1779 in Correggio a decade before
the French Revolution. Ghettos were created over nearly 300
years and varied considerably according to time and place.

The policy of ghettoization was essentially a compromise. Western
Europe, over a period of 200 years, had expelled most of its
Jewish population. By the time of the Venetian ghetto, Britain,
France, many of the Germanic lands, the Low Countries, and
Austria were denuded of a Jewish presence. The expulsion of well
over 50,000 Iberian- or Sephardi-Jews from Spain and its overseas

territories in 1492 (along with their Muslim compatriots) was the last in a long series of expulsions. Forced mass conversion in Portugal in 1497 meant that, after a millennium of co-existence, Jews were no longer able to live on the Iberian peninsula. Unlike the rest of Western Europe (with exceptions such as Frankfurt and Prague), Italy, in its own economic interests, chose the concession of ghettoization, rather than evicting Jews or forcing them to convert to Christianity.

Italy was unique in this regard although the policy of expulsion was still a feature of the region. Spain controlled significant territories in southern Italy, such as Sicily, Naples, and Sardinia, and, as a result, their Jewish populations were expelled in 1492 or soon after. Areas controlled by Venice, Rome, and Florence all compelled Jews to resettle within their territories. This was largely so that Jews, dispersed throughout the peninsula, could be managed and controlled in a few prominent city-states or port cities in northern and central Italy. The result was the wholesale destruction of centuries-old Italian-Jewish communities.

In the context of such devastation, the policy of ghettoization is thought of conventionally as a continuation of medieval anti-Judaism. Sociologist Richard Sennett, for instance, regards the ghetto as an 'urban condom' which protected the Christian population from a noxious Jewish presence which threatened the purity of the Christian message. According to Christian orthodoxy, Jews were unfaithful 'infidels' (as were Moslems) who rejected Catholicism wilfully. They were, as the Italian historian Sara Reguer argues, the equivalent of prisoners, or prostitutes, or the poor, who needed redeeming. The more serious threat to Catholicism were Protestant 'heretics', the main focus of the Roman Inquisition, as they proposed an alternative version of Christianity. That is why potentially redeemable ghettos were often built next to brothels, prisons, and institutions for the destitute.

It is a mystery why it took nearly three centuries to implement the policy of ghettoization if it was an essential means of 'purifying' the nation. One answer is that the creation of ghettos varied considerably throughout Italy and was often at odds with Catholic orthodoxy. While 'purifying' the nation may have been a Roman Catholic prerogative, many city-states prioritized economics over religion. The many hundreds of influential Iberian- and Turkish-Jewish merchants welcomed into city-states in the 16th and 17th centuries confirm the economic imperative. Their presence helps us to understand why the strict policy of ghettoization—'compulsory, segregated and enclosed Jewish quarters'—occurred *en masse* at this time and place, and not before. Christian anti-Judaism does not by itself explain the rise of the ghettos without understanding the economic concerns of the Italian city-states.

Iberian refugees were attracted to Italy due to the similarities between Spanish- and Italian-Jewish cultures. Many of their compatriots migrated to Ottoman-controlled territories in North Africa and the eastern Mediterranean and were hard to distinguish from indigenous 'Levantines'. They were artisans and labourers, and significant numbers had occupational or professional skills—physicians, merchants, pharmacists, bankers—which were much needed in the expanding Ottoman Empire. Their familial and international networks, multilingualism, and perceived religious neutrality, made them invaluable to the mercantile economy between the growing Ottoman Empire and the weakening Italian empires. In the areas controlled by the major city-states, Jewish traders were at the heart of maritime economies. Not unlike the use of district-wide *Fondaci* (or warehouse dwellings) in many Mediterranean port cities, ghettos ensured that taxation and trade (on goods sold and money lent) contributed fully to the government's coffers.

The age of the ghetto pointed both backwards towards past religious orthodoxies and forwards to modern maritime trade.

On the one hand, the Catholic counter-reformation (1545–1648) revitalized medieval Christian anti-Judaism to attack Jews who had yet to convert and recognize Jesus as the messiah. That Jews could move between Moslem, Catholic, and Protestant territories and identities was equally troubling, as the historian E. Natalie Rotham has shown, in an era when religious boundaries (between Catholics and Protestants) were fervently policed. But, at the same time, Italian mercantile economies grew increasingly reliant on Turkish- (or 'Levantine'-) and Iberian- (or 'Ponentine'-) Jewish merchants. Together with local bankers these merchants became an essential source of revenue. But both the theological and economic imperatives were, above all else, a symptom of weakness.

The Catholic counter-reformation was an inherently protective response to the growing power and influence of post-reformation Protestantism. After the Reformation at the beginning of the 16th century, the Catholic Church, buttressed by the Roman Inquisition, returned to first principles. The sacking of Rome in 1527 by German troops stationed in Italy reinforced the vulnerability of the Catholic authorities. Many Protestants supported the attack on Rome which challenged the secular as well as spiritual power of Catholicism. Ghettos were formed in this defensive spirit.

Incorporating Iberian and Levantine merchants into the economy of Italian city-states was also a sign of debilitation. The flatlining economies of the Italian empires, and the failure of young Italian noblemen to engage in mercantile commerce, meant that well-connected cosmopolitan Jewish merchants were much needed. A combination of the Italian Wars fighting off interventions from France, Germany, and Spain–and the external threat from the Ottomans in the East and Atlantic trade in the West—threatened the power of the Italian Empires from the 16th century onwards. It was in the context of the declining economies of the major city-states that ghettos grew in importance over the centuries.

Venice

Up until the later 14th century, when the Venetian Empire was at the height of its power, Jews, with few exceptions, were excluded from the city-state. Instead they lived on the *terra firma* of Mestre, Padua, Verona, and Brescia. This changed in 1509 when the armies of the League of Cambria (an alliance against the Venetian Republic made up of the Holy Roman Empire and Spain) overran the *terra firma*. Around 5,000 refugees fled across the lagoon to the city of Venice which caused food and water shortages and created an unsustainable financial burden. Venice's rivals took advantage of these difficulties to seize as much of its trade as possible.

It was in this weakened state that the ruling Council of Ten, the main governing body in Venice formed in the 14th century, allowed prominent Jewish bankers from Mestre to remain in Venice. After all, enemy soldiers could easily loot their banks on the *terra firma* which was full of Venetian property. Jewish bankers could pay much-needed taxes and were able to keep the high numbers of urban poor from the extremities of impoverishment. Given the vulnerable state of Jewish bankers, the Venetian authorities could ensure that Jews lent to the poor. This contrasted with Christian loan-bankers or *Monti di Pietà*, who tended to be based in Rome, and who charged higher rates than their Jewish counterparts. The Venetian authorities came to value the Jewish bankers from the *terra firma*, not least as the *Monti di Pietà* were much harder to control. Small Jewish bankers from Mestre and elsewhere gradually became de facto confraternities or welfare-providing institutions.

Although the Venetian Republic ordered the refugees from the *terra firma* to leave, after it retook the captured areas in 1515, around 500 Jewish men, women, and children remained in the city. There was an immediate backlash from the Venetian clergy, influenced by the Roman Inquisition, who wanted the remaining Jews, as before, to be expelled. During the heightened emotions of Eastertide they preached sermons against the 'many vices and detestable and abominable things' caused by the Jewish presence in *La Serenissima*. The economic pragmatism of the ruling Council of Ten, if they were to be thought of as god-fearing Catholics, was no longer tenable.

As a compromise between freedom and expulsion, all Jews 'at present living in different parishes within our city' were ordered to reside in the Ghetto Nuovo or 'new foundry'; an island on the northern edges of Venice which had previously been a copper factory. There were just two small bridges to gain access to the island which was ideal for secluding its population (see Figure 2). The Jewish bankers, whose business was on the Rialto, resisted moving to this site but to no avail. A row of modest houses surrounded the pentagon-shaped *piazza* which was thought of

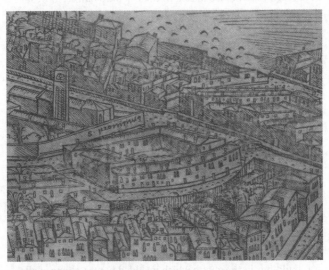

2. **Venice Ghetto (contemporary woodcut).**

as a 'castle' as two high walls were built to close the houses off entirely from the waterfront. The original island had no churches or chapels and was easily guarded and monitored with outward-looking windows bricked up to prevent the viewing of Christian rituals. Two boats, paid for by the residents, patrolled at night-time.

The move to the Ghetto Nuovo took a matter of months with around 700 Italian- and 'German'-Jews (known collectively as *tedeschi*) forced to live in the courtyard and to pay much higher rents than usual to their Christian landlords. There was already a legal basis for a small number of Jews to live temporally in Venice although, before the ghetto, no synagogues were allowed. Jews had long been forbidden sexual and other social relations with Christians and there was extant legislation for them to wear distinguishable yellow hats. But the fundamental change was that Jews were forced to pay four Christian guards to ensure the wooden gates remained locked from dusk until dawn. Above all else, this enforced curfew characterized the Italian ghettos.

The Ghetto Nuovo began precariously with only a five-year license to remain and the threat of expulsion hanging over the residents. But, after a decade of income from the ghetto, the Doge of Venice would not even consider proposals to expel the Jews. The pawnbroker 'banks' and second-hand goods stores (*strazzaria*) were deemed as providing 'money for every need of the State'. These businesses generated exorbitant rates of taxation and paid out many institutional bribes which ensured that they became an essential part of the Venetian micro-economy. As a sign of its success, the numbers in the ghetto began to expand, reaching, at its maximum, nearly 5,000. This expansion caused overcrowding with houses towering higher than any other area in Venice. Precarious floors and walls were added over the years to maximize the sparse land available. After fifty years there were 200 buildings in the ghetto which included homes, shops of all kinds, warehouses, and communal social and religious spaces.

It was a 'Jewish city' in miniature and was treated as such in relation to Venetian law.

The second phase of ghetto expansion took place twenty-five years after the Ghetto Nuovo was formed. In 1541, the Council of Ten invited Levantine-Jewish merchants, who were subjects of the Ottoman Empire, to live in Venice. This was exceptional as only indigenous Venetian merchants could, up to this point, trade with the Ottomans. The Levantines were given unusual trading privileges in wool, silk, and precious metals and were exempted from customs duties. At first, they were asked to live in the original Ghetto Nuova but complained that it was overcrowded. The Venetian authorities eventually agreed that they could reside in an adjacent area known as the Ghetto Vecchio (or old ghetto) built ironically on a new part of the foundry district. The reason why these merchants were granted such extraordinary privileges was that it was believed that trade between Venice, the Balkans, and the Ottoman Empire (close to the Aegean Sea) was in the hands of Levantine-Jewish merchants. Such thinking, however hyperbolic, legitimized the Jewish presence in Venice.

As with the original founding of the ghetto, the Ghetto Vecchio was created at a time when the city-state was weak and in crisis. The Levantines were invited to Venice soon after the conclusion of the third Venetian-Ottoman War (1537–40) which weakened the Republic in the Aegean and Adriatic. At first these merchants were only given a two-year licence to stay and were not allowed to bring their families with them. The Ghetto Vecchio, in other words, was a warehouse dwelling which was the norm for other foreign merchants such as Protestant Germans in the *Fondaco dei Tedeschi*. But the laws prohibiting permanent residence for Levantines, who it was assumed would just house their goods temporarily, were gradually eroded and ignored. Within a few decades, Levantine-Jewish merchants were integral to the Venetian economy and the *Fondaco* became a ghetto. This influence was apparent in 1598 when Daniel Rodriguez, who lived in the Ghetto Vecchio, became the Republic's most powerful agent in Dalmatia.

After a peace treaty with the Ottomans in 1573 the ruling Council of Ten authorized safe-conduct for Spanish- and Portuguese-Jews to settle in Venice in 1589. This was a crucial privilege and was the third and final phase of ghetto expansion. The incorporation of these wealthy merchants into the Venetian economy was part of a wider trend. Other port cities (most notably Venice's direct rival Ancona) not only invited Iberian merchants to settle, but also offered guarantees against persecution. The free port of Livorno soon followed this policy.

Venice could not ignore the presence of these prosperous and influential merchants from Spain and Portugal in rival states. But their presence was ambiguous as they were often Marranos or 'new Christians' (forced converts who continued to practice Judaism in secret). That is why the Venetians categorized these merchants equivocally as 'Ponentines' (a neologism meaning from the West) and ensured their safety as long as they lived as Jews in the ghetto. Venice did participate in the Roman Inquisition (to avoid another war with the Holy Roman Empire) but it did not sacrifice its own commercial and economic interests for religious considerations. The contrast here, as we will see, is with the Papal States who responded severely to 'new Christians' who were deemed to be secret Jews.

The Venetian ghetto was made up of three distinct 'nations' (Germans, Turks, and Spanish) which nonetheless had a collective responsibility in relation to the Venetian authorities. Each of the 'nations' enabled the ghetto to be integrated into the wider economy as separate legal corporations with different trading and economic privileges. The 'Germans' and native Italians were confined to the city-state; the 'Turks' or Levantines were limited to certain trades within the Ottoman Empire; and the 'Spanish' or 'Ponentines' could trade more freely within the Ottoman Empire and Western Europe. Each of these 'nations' built separate institutions—most notably eight synagogues in the ghetto—but paid taxes to the Venetian state as a single entity. The Venetian ghetto was a trinity which acted as one and this model, based on earlier precedents, was replicated throughout most other ghettos.

The creation of the Ghetto Nuovissimo in 1633 for over twenty affluent 'Ponentine'-Jewish families marked a turning point in ghetto development. The Ghetto Nuovissimo was a purely residential district without any businesses and was made up of spacious and elegant houses many of which had direct access to the canal. While the Ghetto Nuovissimo was an extension of the Ghetto Nuovo, it was not part of the original *il terren del geto* or the land of the municipal copper foundry. The word 'ghetto', just over a century after it was first used, no longer referred to a particular location in Venice. After 1633, 'ghetto' was an adjective describing rather opulent houses of wealthy Jewish merchants.

The Ghetto Nuovissimo, for all of its splendour, was also a consequence of instability. The bubonic plague of 1630–1 decimated the population of Venice (relatively less so in the ghetto) and the previous Ottoman War (1570–3) resulted in the loss of Cyprus. By the time of the next Ottoman War (1645–69) Venice was to lose Crete and much of its battle fleet. Venice's position as an international trader, after this war, was fatally weakened with many Jewish traders leaving for Western Europe. But, unlike the Venetians, the Levantine and Ponentine traders had the advantage of being able to engage with both sides of the conflict during the prolonged Ottoman-Venetian Wars. This enabled Jewish traders to increase their role in Venetian shipping which resulted in them owning twelve out of sixty-nine of the largest merchant ships. Their position within a diminished maritime economy, and a less populated ghetto, became more conspicuous. As a result the ghetto as a whole, even with dilapidated accommodation and increased impoverishment, still remained an attractive place to live until its liberation.

Rome

The creation of a second ghetto in Rome in 1555 by Pope Paul IV (1555–9) was the opposite of its precursor in Venice. Whereas Venice incorporated Jews into the local and imperial economy and resisted Papal edicts, Rome, over three centuries, impoverished the Jewish ghetto and supported Christian bankers instead. Jews were treated as an unredeemed people who had yet to see the light. There is much evidence for this polarity. Rome divided up its territories so that the 'economic' ghetto—which incorporated many Levantine and Iberian merchants—was based in Ancona. The Roman ghetto had a diminished economic function and, as a result, was depleted in both 'national' and class terms. This was reflected in the Piazza delle Cinque Scole ('Piazza of the Five Synagogues') which contained each nation in the ghetto (Roman, Spanish, German, Turkish, and Sicilian) in a single building with a modest visage. Unlike Venice, these different Jewish traditions merged through marriage.

In stark contrast to the would-be imperial splendour of the Eternal City, the ghetto had a heightened theological role, for the Papal authorities, as a place of labyrinthine darkness and squalor (see Figure 3). Before his election as Pope Paul IV in 1555, Inquisitor General Cardinale Giovanni Pietro Carafa spearheaded the counter-reformation and led a reinvigorated Roman Inquisition. The papal bull, *Cum Nimis Absurdum* (1555), which inaugurated the Roman ghetto, should be seen in this inquisitorial spirit. The bull was part of a counter-reformation fightback by the Catholic Church and was intended to restore both secular and religious papal authority.

The inhabitants of the Venetian ghetto in 1516 were recent migrants to the city-state having been previously forbidden from living in Venice. But this was not the case in Rome. The vast majority of Roman-Jews were indigenous and could trace their

3. **Rome ghetto (1555–1870).**

genealogy in the Eternal City to the 2nd century BCE. Their daily spoken and written language was Roman dialect and they dressed and ate (albeit according to the laws of *kashrut*) as their Christian neighbours. During ancient and medieval times, the papal authorities had tolerated a Jewish presence based mainly in the Trastevere district of Rome. They were proud to be the oldest Jewish community in the diaspora and felt at home.

Crowds of Roman-Jews, in the decade before the ghetto was created, visited Michelangelo's famous statue of Moses which from 1545 overlooked the grave of Pope Julius II. As the historian Hermann Vogelstein relates, the image of the Roman-Jewish community entering St Peter's Church in Vincoli to see a statue of the Jewish patriarch, which was built on the grave of a Catholic Pope, exemplifies the openness of the Italian Renaissance. A decade later, however, such openness would come to an end.

The creation of the Roman ghetto was one of a series of traumatic events which beset Roman-Jewry from the middle of the 16th century onwards. These events began in 1553 when a Franciscan monk in Rome was accused of promoting Judaism and was consequently burned at the stake. Soon after Jewish homes were ransacked for Hebrew books which, along with the Talmud, were burned on large pyres in Rome and many other Italian cities. After negotiations between rabbinical and papal authorities it was agreed that Jewish religious texts would be self-censured to ensure that they did not 'libel' the Christian Church.

This compromise allowed the self-censured Talmud and other Hebrew books to be printed in Italian states during the age of the ghetto. Italy was, after all, a world centre for Hebrew book printing. But the grim and determined Pope Paul IV was against any form of compromise and on the side of Catholic censorship and torture. It was in this repressive atmosphere that Paul IV, a short time after his election, confined Rome's Jews to the 'Seraglio degli Hebrei' or the 'Enclosure of the Jews'. (The Venetian word 'ghetto' was not in common usage in Rome for another three decades.) As the booming preamble to the Pabal Bull *Cum Nimis Absurdum* makes clear, the proud and ancient Roman-Jewish community was to be utterly enclosed:

> As it is completely absurd and improper that the Jews, condemned by God to eternal servitude because of guilt, should, on the pretext that they are accepted by Christian piety and permitted to live in our midst, be so ungrateful to Christians as to insult them for their mercy and presume to superiority instead of the subjection that they deserve; and because we have been informed that in Rome and elsewhere their insolence is such that they presume to live among Christians in the neighbourhood of churches without distinction of dress.

Cum Nimis Absurdum returns to medieval precepts ('distinctions of dress') as well as urban planning ('[Jews] presume to live among Christians'). The area chosen as the Jewish *Seraglio*, the district of Sant'Angelo (the smallest district in Rome), on the east bank of the Tiber, housed 80 per cent of the Jewish community. But the remaining population, including wealthy bankers, had long since moved beyond this relatively poor area, which was built on a flood plain with overspilling sewage. They moved outside of Sant'Angelo into more desirable districts which had no previous Jewish residents. But, within a month, all Jews were forced to wear distinguishing yellow clothing and, with unprecedented speed, were herded together into their *Seraglio*. Within two months the walls surrounding Sant'Angelo enclosed an overcrowded 7 acre accretion of winding narrow streets for a population of around 2,500 people.

The ghetto was roughly rectangular with two main streets running parallel to the Tiber. Walls were quickly constructed between houses which were connected by narrow alleyways and four small squares but, unlike Venice, no large central *piazza*. Piazza Giudea, the site of a market, was cut in two and was on the edge of the ghetto. The ghetto was overcrowded from the start but became inhumanly so after nearly 1,000 refugees expelled from the Papal States came to Rome in the 1570s. Only one entrance and exit was allowed although more were created as buildings were added to the ghetto.

As specified in the bull, all Jews were forced to sell their property (at a quarter of its value) including those who already resided in Sant'Angelo. The bull also reinstituted many medieval restrictions against Jews which were first introduced at the long-forgotten Fourth Lateran Council (1215). These constraints included eating with Christians, employing Christian servants, and limiting work to that of second-hand goods ('strazzaria'). Such restrictions were more severe than the Venetian ghetto especially when it came to draconian rules covering banking, the constraint on Jewish doctors treating Christian patients, and the proscription on Jews trading in foodstuffs. The papal control over Rome's Jews was complete.

The Papal States covered an area greater than any other Italian government. Local rulers used *Cum Nimis Absurdum* as an excuse to imprison, forcibly convert, or impoverish their Jewish communities, and many Jews fled north to more tolerant cities such as Urbino or Ferrara. But it was Ancona which bore the brunt of Pope Paul IV's punitive new policy against the Jews.

As part of their economic pragmatism, his predecessors, Paul III (1534–49) and Pope Julius III (1550–5), had invited 'all merchants of whatever nation, faith or sect, even if Turks, Jews, or other infidels' to come to Ancona. The Adriatic port of Ancona was located 160 miles north of Venice. It was the main source of maritime wealth for the Papal States and competed directly with its Venetian neighbour. Paul IV's predecessors also specified that Portuguese Marranos ('of Jewish origin called new Christians') were welcome in Ancona. It was this policy that was emulated by Venice who accepted 'Ponentine' merchants into the ghetto. But, nine months after his election, Paul IV unexpectedly reversed the papal protection of 'new Christians' who were said to have reverted to Judaism from Christianity. In April 1556, he encouraged the Inquisition to arrest around one hundred 'Marrano' Turkish- and Iberian-Jews who, by rejecting their baptism, were accused of heresy.

As most of those arrested had strong links with the Ottoman Empire, a delegation from Ancona was sent to the Jewish leader Dona Gracia Mendes, the Marrano *grande dame* and business magnate who had moved from Ferrara to Constantinople. She was a formidable leader who enlisted the support of the Ottoman sultan, Suleiman the Magnificent, who advised the pope to free all Jews who were Ottoman subjects as he could not otherwise guarantee the safety of Christians within his empire.

One-third of the arrested Marranos were released; one-third repudiated their 'return' to Judaism; but twenty-five refused to admit to being heretics. This latter group of Marrano 'Jews' were burned at the stake in June 1556 in a notorious *auto-da-fé*. In response to this outrage, the redoubtable Dona Gracia worked with the sultan to organize a blockade of the port of Ancona. The Turkish navy was placed in the Adriatic close to Ancona but, after nearly two years, Ancona's Jewish merchants appealed to Dona Gracia to end the boycott as it was bankrupting many of them. In the coming decades, Ancona proved essential to the papal maritime economy which competed vigorously with Venice and Livorno. The demonstration of the close ties between the Jews of Ancona and Constantinople, in instigating the boycott, resulted paradoxically in the eventual incorporation of many wealthy Levantine and Iberian merchants.

When the unpopular Paul IV died Roman citizens celebrated with the head of his statue being dragged around and used as a football. He is universally regarded as one of the most brutal and reactionary popes in history. But *Cum Nimis Absurdum* did act as a point of continuity over the next two centuries for future popes to incorporate the ghetto into the urban landscape of north-central Italy. This was especially true after the accession of Pope Pius V (1566–72), another former inquisitor general, who in 1569 issued the papal bull *Hebraeorum Gens*. This ordered Jews living in nearly eighty cities and towns of the Papal States—such as Bologna, Benevento, Camerino, and Fano—to leave for either Rome or Ancona within three months or their possessions would be confiscated. In Bologna, for instance, when the 900-year-old flourishing Jewish community was ended, bodies were removed from the Jewish cemetery to be reburied elsewhere.

The Papal States covered the whole of central Italy—Campania, Romagna, Ancona, and most of Umbria—and included more Jews than the rest of the peninsula. This meant that around 7,000 people were turned into refugees with many leaving the Papal States at the risk of death, impoverishment, or imprisonment. Following the expulsion of the Jews in the Kingdom of Naples in 1541, this policy was the closest that Italy came to emulating the rest of Western Europe.

Less severe popes, such as Pope Sixtus V (1585–90)—who expanded the ghetto and eased some of the harsher restrictions on Jews—were no less blinkered than their hard-line predecessors. As part of Sixtus's purging of Rome's slums, he reintegrated the ghetto into the urban landscape as he recognized that the conditions of the muddy coastal strip on the east bank of the Tiber were overcrowded and insanitary. But this piecemeal expansion was not purely altruistic as his sister benefited from unregulated ghetto rents.

Sixtus V is well known for introducing iconic Roman boulevards and radial streets to highlight the power and authority of 'Roma Christiana'. His modernization of Rome, with its imposing ceremonial vistas, united its imperial past with its contemporary incarnation as a spiritual empire. In this context the streets connected to the ghetto, and the newly constructed buildings on the banks of the Tiber, incorporated the ghetto more firmly into Rome's imperial iconography. It was at this point, in 1589, that ghetto residents recognized that theirs was a site of utter powerlessness and they started using the term 'ghetto' (rather than *Seraglio*) in an ironic reference to the Hebrew word 'ghet' or 'bill of divorce'. The original Venetian etymology now merged with Hebrew. After nearly two millennia, the Roman-Jewish community was forced to recognize that it was finally 'divorced' from the rest of Rome.

A fountain, located in Piazza Mattei since the beginning of the 17th century, ensured some access to fresh water. As with the Venetian ghetto, one solution to the overcrowding was to add many floors, and also to split rooms into two or three, in the Roman tenement houses. But these jerry-built tenements did not prevent several families sleeping in a crowded annex, or in rotation, and resulted in regular building accidents (most notoriously on one occasion killing many wedding guests). Windows overlooking Rome (again emulating Venice) were bricked off. Rents were eventually fixed by their Christian owners according to the Jewish tradition of *jus hazaqa* (right of possession), an agreed practice across all ghettos, which meant that Jews could not be evicted from their homes by the owners.

Rome has entered the popular imagination as the archetypal ghetto associated with flooding, sewage, poverty, and overcrowding. Ferdinand Gregorovius, the German historian of medieval Rome, witnessed the last two decades of the ghetto in the 1850s and reflected what many earlier visitors had reported:

> When I first visited [the ghetto] the Tiber had overflowed its banks and the yellow flood streamed through the Fiumara, the lowest of the ghetto streets, the foundations of whose houses stand partly in the water.... Each year Israel in Rome has to undergo a new deluge.

An overflowing Tiber routinely flooded the first floor of the many houses closest to the river. This was a common problem in Rome. But the impoverished ghetto exacerbated such acts of nature. A contemporary Italian observer described the ghetto as a 'formless heap of hovels and dirty cottages, ill kept, in which a population of four thousand souls vegetates, when half that number could with difficulty live there'.

The success of Ancona meant that the Roman ghetto was primarily a means of humiliating its residents so that they would eventually convert and be part of 'Roma Christiana'. That is why Jewish loan banks, the economic engine of most Italian-Jewish communities, were closed in Rome in 1682 and replaced entirely with their Christian equivalent. All that was left was the poor-man's trade in second-hand goods. Even this lowly trade was resented as rag-based paper made out of cloth was increasingly used. Deprivation led to many ghetto shops providing furnishings (beds, mattresses, clothing, curtains) for nearby brothels and criminal gangs. Gregorovius witnessed the scene of this impoverishment: 'the world seems to lie about, transformed into Jewish trash, tattered and torn, in countless rags and scraps. Pieces of junk of every kind and colour are heaped high before the doors'. No wonder the plague of 1656 killed 800, nearly a quarter of the ghetto's population.

The ruinous taxes (which included paying for the annual right to live in the ghetto and the maintenance of the nearby Jewish cemetery) made little economic sense. Jews also had to pay for the *Casa dei catecumeni* (the 'house of converts'), which they were compelled to visit outside of the ghetto to undergo baptism. But such impoverishment reflected the decline of Rome as a whole. The imperial ambition of its absolutist papal authorities was in stark contrast to its depleted resources. In this context, the symbolic role of the ghetto as a place of subjection and profanity was paramount. This perception was reinforced with the help of weekly conversion sermons, humiliating rituals at carnivals and elsewhere, regular plays mocking Jews and Judaism, and daily violence against ghetto residents. Out of a final population of 4,500 in 1870, before the ghetto was liberated, only 200 had sufficient means to pay the requisite taxes, keep the ghetto infrastructure working, and provide for those who were most in need.

That only a relatively small percentage of Roman-Jews converted after three centuries of severe coercion points to a paradox of ghettoization. The Roman ghetto was under direct control of the papal authorities, which meant that Jewish rulers in the ghetto had to use a Christian legal system. Segregation led to acculturation. By denying the Jewish community any self-government, even abolishing Jewish notaries, the papal authorities in effect ensured that Roman-Jews were fully integrated into the wider culture. There was, in other words, no need for Jews to convert to become full citizens.

Legally all ghettos were collectives (*universita ebrai*) and were rightly described as 'Jewish cities'. In Rome, the lack of any autonomy meant that a tight-knit communal identity often took a spiritual form or holy community (*Kehillot Kadoshot*). The necessary use of the synagogue for all secular and religious activities reinforced this sense of abiding spirituality. This was a common response to ghettoization and resulted in a rich Kabbalistic and Rabbinic tradition.

Florence

The ghetto formed in 1571 in the heart of Florence has some similarities with both Rome and Venice. But, like all Italian ghettos, the Florentine ghetto was primarily a product of its local conditions. Pope Pius V expelled Jews from the Papal States in 1569 with the exception of Rome and Ancona. These states included most of Umbria which resulted in a flow of refugees northwards into Tuscany. This immediate context was the catalyst for new ghettos in Florence in 1571 and Siena in 1572.

Cosimo de' Medici (1537–74), the first Grand Duke of Tuscany, had revived the Florentine economy, honed its bureaucracy, and welcomed Levantine-Jews from the Ottoman Empire. All of this statecraft was designed to consolidate the Medici's power after years of internal strife caused by the Italian Wars, devastating plagues, and economic stagnation. Cosimo needed to demonstrate that his well-ordered state was able to manage the homelessness caused by *Hebraeorum Gens*. Only Pope Pius V could appoint him as Grand Duke, which was why Cosimo had to have a good relationship with him. Given the continued conflicts between Turkey, the Italian city-states, France, and Spain, Cosimo also needed to be perceived to be a strong Christian leader within the Holy Roman Empire.

In September 1570, Cosimo issued an edict which expelled around 700 Jews who were dispersed in sundry villages and towns under his control. Not unlike *Hebraeorum Gens* Jews were compelled to leave the Florentine Dominion but were given 'full license' to live in either Florence or Siena as long as it was in 'such streets and places that will be declared'. Unlike the focus on conversion in Rome, Cosimo did not build a *Casa dei Catecumeni* for compulsory Christian instruction in the ghetto. A house of conversion, which Venice introduced in 1557, was not built in Florence until 1636. The Florentine ghetto also differed from Venice as Cosimo did not renew the licences of Jewish loan-bankers who had helped to restore the economy in the Medici State. As a consequence, established loan-bankers refused to move to the Florentine ghetto. To solve this lacuna Cosimo's son Ferdinando de Medici (1587–1609) formed a purely economic ghetto in Livorno and Pisa in 1593.

The Florentine ghetto, unlike the extremes of Rome and Venice, proved to be the model for most subsequent ghettos in northern Italy. It was essentially a form of profitable urban renewal with Cosimo focusing on a run-down area of central Florence: a rectangle of approximately 100 by 200 yards. Most of the area already had high walls as it included Florence's main brothels. Cosimo purchased tenement houses, shops, warehouses, modest homes occupied by prostitutes, as well as the grander homes of more noble families. The town centre was swiftly transformed so as to contain a captured population of 700 people who were forced to pay high rents to the leader of the Medici State. There was a curfew, compulsory yellow clothing (the same colour that prostitutes wore), only two gates to enter and exit, and a nearby Jewish cemetery. Many of the shops and some of the houses were of a high quality. After Venice, Rome, and Ancona, the Florentine ghetto exemplified the strength of the Medici's leaders who were shaping Florence in their own image.

The ghetto, in other words, was a form of well-regulated government which could be projected throughout the Papal States and the Holy Roman Empire. In 1572, the ghetto in Siena was formed again with only two gates. It was based around an established infrastructure with a shopping market, unlike Florence, and a different non-Medici administration. Built in the centre of Siena around the ancient synagogue, the ghetto was always small (no more than a few hundred residents) and was close to the main Piazza del Campo. Siena became known as Little Jerusalem (a Holy Community) because of its five rabbinical schools, a prominent statue of Moses, and a nearby purifying fountain. Residents were able to study medicine at the local university following the many Venetian-Jews who obtained medical degrees from Padua. All, apart from the physicians, wore yellow and all in the ghetto paid a special tax, newly established high rents, and were restricted to certain trades which would aid the local economy but not disadvantage their Christian competitors.

Livorno and Pisa were exceptions to the typical ghetto formation in Florence and Siena. They were free ports or merchant colonies designed to attract Spanish-, Portuguese-, and Turkish-Jews. In an astonishing act of foresight, Ferdinando Medici also granted generous rights and privileges to English merchants as Livorno had relatively easy access to Western Europe and the Atlantic. The Adriatic Ports of Venice and Ancona were immediately disadvantaged. As a result Livorno thrived. After modernizing the Livorno harbour at great expense, and making it an attractive place to live for wealthy merchants, Ferdinando issued the *Livorniana* invitation in 1593. This was a series of charters and privileges to 'merchants of whatever nation' (although aimed specifically at Levantines and Iberians) to settle.

The only other ghetto in the Medici State was formed in Pitigliano in 1622. This was also known as Little Jerusalem because of the relatively large number of Jews—when compared to the overall population—which found refuge from the extremities of the nearby Papal States. Jews on the peninsula, who were always on the move, now understood the various kinds of ghettos, economic or religious, tolerant or intolerant, in the different city-states.

The privileges granted to Livorno in particular were extraordinarily generous. Venice was forced to follow suit with the creation of the Ghetto Nuovissimo for wealthy 'Ponentines' in 1633. Ferdinando's aim was to make Livorno the merchant capital of the Medici State and also to compete with the ports of Trieste, Amsterdam, and London as well as his declining Italian rivals. In this he was conspicuously successful. Pisa remained a cultural centre for its established Jewish community, but wealthy merchants preferred Livorno and the relative freedom from religious authorities of all kinds.

The last ghettos formed on the peninsula—Vercelli (1724), Acqui (1731), Moncalvo (1732), Correggio (1779)—were ruled by the Piedmont government in north-west Italy. Eighteenth-century ghettos followed the irresistible expansion of ghettoization in Venetian towns on the *terra firma*—Verona (1597), Padua (1603), Rovigo (1615), Conigliano (1675)—and especially in the expanded Papal States—Ferrara (1627), Lugo (1634), and Cento (1636). Together with indigenous Italians who were part of centuries-old communities, refugees from as far afield as the Levant, Iberia, and Western Europe could be found in the larger ghettos (over a few thousand occupants) such as Verona, Padua, and Ferrara. Smaller ghettos (under 500) tended to be built around a local synagogue, a family of loan-bankers, and extant communities over many centuries.

The late flourish of ghettoization on the peninsula in the 17th and 18th centuries was close enough to the modern period to highlight the many contradictions in ghetto formation. On the one hand, the ghettos in the Veneto and Piedmont regions succumbed to ever more anxious and extreme papal pressure (based on increasingly severe accounts of Jews and Judaism) as a counter to enlightenment values. Good relations with Rome often included the introduction of a ghetto even for a few hundred people. But ghettoization was also a product of modernity, as the Florentine ghettos established with regard to urban planning and, as Pisa and Livorno illustrated, with regard to a thriving mercantile economy. Outside of the control of the Holy See, ghettoized Jews were treated as a modern community of citizens who paid taxes according to their specific trading activities and answered directly to the local authorities.

Most ghettos had some form of social and religious autonomy or 'corporate governing organisation' according to the influential Jewish historian Salo Baron. That is why ghettos were treated legally as cities made up of merchant guilds. Jews were responsible for sanitation, water, policing, and fire prevention along with the daily running of the ghetto. The vast majority of older ghettos, especially by the 18th century, were overtaxed, impoverished, and overcrowded. But ghetto assemblies, for the most part, regulated what each member had to pay to the ruling authorities. Much of the flourishing cultural life of the ghetto resulted from this autonomy and such self-government often proved popular. When the Ghetto of Verona was formed in 1597, after much delay, there was a public celebration to welcome the 'camp of the Hebrews'.

One aspect of ghettoization followed the reactionary policies of the counter-reformation—including papal inquisitions, *autos-da-fé*, the burning of Jewish religious books, and the summary killing of heretics. But ghettoization also pointed in the direction of a modern maritime economy and new forms of urban spatial management and welfare provision. No ghetto imprisoned Jews even if they were sometimes predicated on a conversionist zeal which treated Jews as prisoners in need of redemption. That Jews were under curfew and lived in a walled 'city' was not unique and was comparable with foreign merchants who lived in similarly curfewed warehouse dwellings, or nuns or prostitutes or the poor who were thoroughly scrutinized in often nearby enclosed buildings. The age of the ghetto, although deeply influenced by medieval Jewish quarters, helped to shape the modern and contemporary world as both history and myth; precedent and symbol. That is why a purely sorrowful account of this complex and contradictory epoch, as the historian David Ruderman rightly argues, is wide of the mark.

This chapter has stressed the power of local governments to shape the Italian ghettos in their own image. But that does not mean that Jews did not have access to the wider culture. The economic context of the larger ghettos was international in nature and transcended the Catholic Church. As a result this context gave rise to a vibrant secular culture which women in particular could contribute too as writers, teachers, communal leaders, and even *Kosher* butchers. This culture included books on theology, literature, music, science, and medicine all of which were disseminated throughout Europe in unique Hebrew typeface. Out of the ghetto came such luminaries as the physician Azariah de'Rossi (1511–78), the leading composer Salomone de' Rossi (1570–1630), the polymath Leone da Modena (1571–1648), the poets Sara Coppio Sullan (1592–1641) and Leone de Sommi (1527–92), and the dramatist Jacob Zahalon (1630–93). Each of these figures could be multiplied many times over. For nearly three centuries, song, poetry, music, philosophy, and drama were all part of ghetto life.

The age of the ghetto, as the Jewish historian Robert Bonfil has noted, was just as intellectually liberating and culturally creative for Italian-Jews as the years of the preceding Italian Renaissance. Certainly an unparalleled number of Jewish physicians were produced during these years. Rabbis and communal leaders often had medical or philosophical degrees, and all were conversant in Italian as well as Jewish literature and science. They were to pass their vast knowledge on to those who lived in the ghetto and they also taught in Jewish religious seminaries ('Yeshivas') within the ghetto. It is for this reason that Baron has rejected a purely 'lachrymose' account of ghetto life which, he rightly argues, is a product of present-day distortions of the historic Italian ghettos which began in the 19th century.

Chapter 3
Ghettos of the imagination

At the end of the 18th century, Napoleon Bonaparte's troops abolished settlement restrictions after entering the western part of the Holy Roman Empire and Northern Italy. In French-controlled areas, Jews and other minorities were immediately granted civil rights. The wooden gates of Italian ghettos were ceremoniously removed and burned so as to give these historic ghettos a lasting symbolic meaning. They were, after all, the very opposite of the enlightened nation-state and associated irrevocably with a bygone past. The 'Age of the Ghetto' had come to an end and the modern era was born.

The Rome ghetto was finally freed in 1870 with the demise of the Papal States and the unification of Italy. Up until that point the many travellers who visited Rome on the Grand Tour witnessed the degradation of the ghetto, and associated it with an unenlightened and primitive past. It was regularly under water, as it was built on a flood plain, and filled with foul-smelling debris. Nothing could have contrasted more with the grandeur and purity of Rome. Soon after the new Italian nation-state was formed, the ghetto was demolished and Jews were granted full citizenship. By 1904, an imposing synagogue was built at the heart of the old ghetto to confirm that Jews, along with other minorities, were equal citizens under the law. The Rome ghetto, along with its 18th-century counterparts, was finally consigned to the dustbin of history.

Throughout the 19th century, as Jews strived for emancipation throughout the German lands of Western Europe, the ghetto was perceived as the very opposite of modern citizenship. It became a free-floating concept as Jews and other minorities were expected to acculturate into mainstream German society by disavowing particularism ('the ghetto') in the name of a transformative German culture or 'bildung'. Germany, following Italy, became a unified nation-state in 1871. Jewish emancipation was not granted in every state until this point as German civil servants often made full citizenship contingent on a community's Germanization (language, dress, location). The ghetto, from this perspective, represented social isolation and an outmoded Judaism. German modernizers (both Jews and Christians) thought of emancipation as the inverse of ghettoization.

Soon after historic ghettos were closed, the word 'ghetto' was circulated widely (beyond its historic Italian origins) initially in the German language, then in French, English, Dutch, Yiddish, Hebrew, Russian, and Polish. In the 1840s, German novelists invented a new genre of ghetto stories (or *Gettogeschichten*). This popular genre located the idea of the ghetto in the past and on the eastern borders of the Prussian State. Every Central European 'Jewish alley' (*Judengasse*), however small and inconsequential, became a ghetto overlain with poetic, spiritual, and, most often, feminized values. They could not have contrasted more with the thrusting masculinized modernity of the progressive nation-state.

Following the destruction of actual ghettos, the imagined ghetto had a rich afterlife. As soon as Jews were free to live in Western Europe, the concept of the ghetto became a way of considering what kind of citizens Jews would become in a Christian nation-state. Jews of the ghetto were thought to oppose progress which meant that they had to leave it twice over. They left once in actuality, and again symbolically by becoming acculturated. No wonder Jewish novelists wished to offer a counter-narrative so that they could portray the ghetto as a space for authentic Jewish practices to be valued. The spiritual ghetto, a welcome alternative to modernity, remained an attractive concept for European Jews throughout the 19th century.

When decoupled from actual locations, the free-floating ghetto ranged widely. Within a century the word travelled East to encompass Jewish townships (*shtetls*) and the Pale of the Settlement (the region where most Jews lived in Imperial Russia). By the second half of the 19th century, it crossed the Atlantic to the United States (via German-Jewish immigrants) to account for new areas of urban Jewish settlement. The word 'ghetto' often referred to actual places in Italy, Germany, and Spain, but it could also just be a state of mind (commonly referred to as a 'ghetto mentality' or a form of diaspora timidity). The spaces which were deemed to be 'ghettos' quickly multiplied. While imagined ghettos were firmly located in the rural past, they did not remain there for long. By the 1890s the idea of the ghetto in Britain, Western Europe, and North America was to be firmly rooted in the urban present.

Germany

The word 'ghetto' (or 'getto') entered the German language in the 17th century but referred only to Italian ghettos. The Frankfurt *Judengasse* (1462–1811) had the same characteristics as the major Italian ghettos but was not called a 'ghetto' and was generally grouped together with other European Jewish quarters or Jewish streets ('Judenquartiers', 'Judenstrasse'). This is clear from the second chapter of Heinrich Heine's unfinished novel *The Rabbi of Bacherach* (*Der Rabbi von Bacherach*) begun in 1824 and partly finished in 1840. In his account of the Frankfurt *Judengasse* Heine anticipates the ambivalence of much German ghetto literature without calling the *Judengasse* a 'ghetto'. The *Judengasse* is both 'a horrifying memorial to the Middle Ages' but also a place of authentic Jewish spirituality ('those ancient solemn chants') and a monument to Jewish survival ('a martyrdom that lasted a thousand years'). This mixture of disgust and reverence was typical of much German-Jewish ghetto literature.

The first German book with the word 'ghetto' in the title was Berthold Auerbach's *The Ghetto* (*Das Ghetto*) which collected two novels *Spinoza* (1837) and *Poet and Merchant* (*Dichter and Kaufmann*; 1840). As with *The Rabbi of Bacherach* this collection was unfinished as if the many meanings of 'ghetto' could not yet be accounted for. But what was significant about Auerbach's collection was its preface which associated 'the ghetto' in general with Jewish traditions and customs. No longer associated with a particular place, the ghetto became a generalized descriptive term which, in Auerbach's words, 'endures until today'. As Heine anticipated, Jewish ritual objects and artefacts, biblical themes, scenes from Jewish religious life, decorative dress, pewter plates, all became a form of 'ghetto nostalgia' in historian Richard Cohen's resonant phrase (see Figure 4). The ghetto was turned into a space of innate spirituality and kinship which was under threat from a modern, increasingly urbanized, nation-state.

Heine and Auerbach were two of the most widely read writers in 19th-century Germany. Their brief sojourn in the world of the ghetto was influential and was quickly taken up by Leopold Kompert (1822–86), who wrote extensively about the Bohemian *Judengasse* of his youth as if it were a memoir of a 'ghetto'. Heine returned to poetry and Auerbach quickly became known for his bestselling *Black Forest Village Tales* (*Schwarzwälder Dorfgeschichten*; 1843). These tales were extraordinarily popular in Germany as they unified imaginatively the nation. Auerbach's portrait of the timeless dignity, authenticity, and humanity of provincial life, in the context of increased urbanization and rapid social change, were read throughout Europe. *Villages Tales* was translated into virtually every European language. George Eliot in England and George Sand in France, for instance, took up Auerbach's themes in their rural fiction published in the 1850s and 1860s.

4. *The Volunteer* (1834) **by Moritz Daniel Oppenheim.**

Kompert was particularly influenced by *Village Tales* and soon became known as 'The Auerbach of the Ghetto'. His sentimental version of the ghetto, set in rural Bohemia, was full of local colour, timeless social types, and spiritual values that contrasted starkly with modernization. Kompert inaugurated the genre of ghetto literature, based on Auerbach's stories, and was the self-designated 'poet of the ghetto' (a phrase which followed him throughout the century). He wrote four influential volumes of ghetto stories and four novels beginning with *Scenes from the Ghetto* (*Aus dem Ghetto*; 1848) and ending with his eighth book, *Franzi and Heini, a Viennese History* (*Franzi und Heini, eine Wiener Geschichte*; 1880).

While Kompert claimed a personal connection to the Bohemian ghetto, he attended the universities in Prague and Vienna and lived mainly in Vienna, even serving on the city council. He was, above all, a mediator who could portray his imagined ghettos so that middle-class German-Jews were able to reconcile their Germanness and Jewishness, emancipation and the ghetto, the secular and the spiritual. Such mediation is first seen in the visionary prologue of Kompert's *Scenes from the Ghetto* entitled 'Outside the Ghetto'. The narrator remembers how, as a boy, he defied his grandparents and climbed a 'mountain' (at least from his boyish perspective) outside the *Judengasse*. He recounts his act of rebellion with the following:

> [My grandparents] had warned me, they had urged me not to go, not to take this dangerous path up the mountain; but I had laughed at them and said: Let me go! And now I stood up there. My grandmother is wringing her hands in anguish…and my grandfather is wagging his finger and shaking his head thoughtfully.

The prologue ends with the boy crying out 'Let me go! On the mountain I must stand!' which dramatizes the boy's physical and intellectual transcendence of the ghettoized Jewish world. The curiosity of the young boy, exploring the wider world beyond the ghetto boundaries, culminates in him rejecting the world of his grandparents. His viewpoint on high clearly stands for the narrative position of Kompert who, like the grandson, writes his subsequent stories detached from the ghetto. He is the 'poet of the ghetto' because he sentimentalizes his subject (following Schiller) as an idealized lost world. Such longing for the ghetto, articulated through his acculturated characters, spoke specifically to Kompert's acculturated German-Jewish readers.

Kompert writes in German from Vienna rather than in Yiddish from Bohemia, and with a university rather than a rabbinic education. All of his stories highlight the foreignness of the Yiddish language and Jewish customs, and the distance between these and his intended German readership. On the first page of *Scenes from the Ghetto* he speaks on behalf of his readers' 'servants', which locates his readership in a particular social class. According to the narrator, only 'your servant' knows what the 'true meaning' of the equally lowly 'schlemiel' (or village idiot) is.

'Schlemiel' is the first of Kompert's stories and sets the scene for the rest of the book by characterizing the fool as the reverse of the usurious money-lender: 'put gold into the hand of the schlemiel and...he will change it into copper; give him copper and he will turn it into lead, unfit even to make a bullet for blowing out one's brains'. The desperate fate of the 'schlemiel' is unremitting and leads (as the story anticipates) to his suicide. Kompert generates an abiding sympathy for such downwardly mobile figures in stark contrast to his upwardly mobile readership.

The transitional nature of Kompert's fiction should not be underestimated. The recovery of invented ghettos in Middle Europe, in Bohemia, is of particular significance in this regard. The Jewish communities of his native Bohemia, after all, are somewhere between an emancipated Western Jewry and traditional Jewish *shtetl*-life in Eastern Europe. This explains the doubleness of Kompert's stories with many of his characters leaving the ghetto only to be compelled to return by a potent sense of organic connection: 'In the Ghetto every individual is bound by a thousand chains to the community'.

In 'The Pedlar' (1849), for instance, the prodigal son returns from university to the ghetto disguised as a pedlar, which is his father's occupation. The son wishes to marry a Christian woman but is overwhelmed by the strong emotional bonds to his family and community personified by his eponymous father. An authentic sense of belonging, a common suffering, and conventional family values, enables Kompert's ghetto stories to mediate between a vanishing Jewish particularity (especially with regard to the acculturating Jewish middle classes) and the German nation as a whole.

Kompert first popularized European ghetto fiction (as well as the word ghetto) in the mid-19th century. He is often compared to his younger friend and protégé Karl Emil Franzos (1848–1904) who was born in Galicia, lived in Vienna, Budapest, and Berlin, and went to the universities of Vienna and Gratz. Franzos, who claimed a superior Sephardi (Iberian) heritage—a higher class when compared to East Europeans—is rightly described as the negative 'intellectual scion of Kompert'. He largely denigrates the Barnow Ghetto, which is the fictional name of Franzos's native Czortków, a small town where the Austro-Hungarian and Russian empires met. Franzos describes Barnow as 'a squalid nook in a God-forgotten corner of the earth, where the great current of life hardly seems to cause the faintest ripple'. No longer is the ghetto, and by extension rural East-Central Europe, sentimentalized as pre-modern. Instead it returns to the present and becomes a 'dark place' in need of 'as much light' as possible.

The revolutionary year of 1848 is a crucial context for both Kompert's and Franzos's ghetto fiction. Kompert reinforces the revolutionary precepts of 1848. He follows earlier papal teachings and revolutionary projections, and devises stories about ghetto Jews as prospective farmers and tillers of the soil or, at least, as manual labourers. But Franzos is writing in the late 1860s and 1870s, two decades later, when the promise of radical change had been thwarted. His account of the ghetto is far more sombre and acerbic.

The difference between Kompert and Franzos is summarized in Franzos's 1877 preface to *The Jews of Barnow*, where he refers to ghetto life, as described in his collection of stories, as a 'strange life', and goes on: 'I am conscious of the fact that I have described this strange life in the way it appeared to me'. In his 1893 introduction to his novel *The Pojaz* (or 'The Clown') he writes against Kompert: 'The poetic aspect of much of Judaism's forms did not escape me, but their charm can be fully felt only by those to whom they convey some childhood memories. That was not my case'. In his no holds barred obituary of the older writer, Franzos explicitly distances himself from his mentor. According to Franzos, 'Jewish life, as portrayed by Kompert, appears more edifying than it really is'.

Franzos was writing not merely as a detached outsider (after Kompert) but as a German writer who found the ghetto 'strange', who had a didactic programme of Germanization which he promoted in his fiction, and who described Polish Galicia and the surrounding regions as 'half-Asian' (the title of his first 1876 collection). The orientalism of Franzos presumed that ghettoized Jews were a 'dirty', backward people desperately in need of the values of the Western Enlightenment:

> What a peculiar history the Jews have had! Their strong religion, founded on a rock was once a protection to them, and saved them from their enemies.... But now, when the light of day is shining in the West, and the dawn has broken in the East... I only desire that they should open their eyes to the light which is shining more and more around them.

The Jews of Eastern Europe were 'half-Asian' because they lived in supposedly barbaric conditions. If Polish Jews were to be the equal of their German compatriots then they would have to live somewhere which was more cultivated. That was why Franzos famously said in his preface to *The Jews of Barnow*: 'Every country gets the Jews it deserves'. He goes on to say, 'It is not the fault of Polish Jews that they are less civilized than their brethren in the faith in England, Germany and France. At least it is not entirely their fault'. Only by moving to Western Europe could Jews become more 'civilized'.

Here Franzos was no different than German-language authors in general, such as the peculiarly philosemitic Leopold von Sacher-Masoch who described the 'Polish ghetto', in his words, as a 'miniature Orient in the Middle of Europe'. Whereas

Kompert thought of rural life as a means of redeeming ghettoized Jews, Franzos described the so-called 'half-Asian' regions of Galicia as an anonymous and characterless blot on the landscape. Geography itself was ghettoized from this orientalist perspective with the wind sounding 'like a sigh of a weary spirit when it swept over the desolate field'. No longer was an imagined village-like ghetto able to redeem the modern world. Instead, the books of Franzos were taken up by racial anti-Semites who agreed that ghettoized Jews were irredeemably different to 'Aryan' Western peoples. Unlike German-Jewish authors who believed in the emancipatory project, such racial anti-Semites argued that all Jews were oriental strangers ('half-Asian') not just those who lived in ghettos.

France

Ghetto fiction in France directly followed the fiction of Auerbach and Kompert. This can be seen especially in the work of Alexandre Weill (1811–99) who was born in a small Jewish village in French-ruled Alsace. He was a friend of Heine and Auerbach and claimed to have invented the 'village tale' in the 1830s before George Sand. His village tales, in contrast to Auerbach's, began with traditional Alsatian-Jewish life which was on the verge of extinction rather than an example of pre-modern values. He wrote initially in German and then in French, and wavered, bizarrely, between revolutionary and reactionary politics.

Weill's stories perceived Paris as the 'new Jerusalem' in contrast to his fictionalized Alsatian ghettos. His characters leave their villages for Paris and, unlike Kompert's narratives, were no longer drawn back to the spiritual community of their upbringing. The Judaism of Weill's younger characters was reformed (based on rationality as much as faith) in line with the revolutionary values of the French republic. The adaptation of ghetto literature to the ethos of post-revolutionary France can be contrasted with the fiction of Daniel Stauben (born Auguste Widel) who followed

Kompert more straightforwardly. This is not surprising as Stauben was Kompert's French translator in the 1850s and 1860s.

Born in Alsace, Stauben's *Letters on Alsatian Manners* (*Lettres sur les moeurs Alsciennes*; 1849) portrayed the 'antique simplicity' of semi-rural Alsatian-Jewish life which supposedly acted as a sanctuary from the revolutionary year which preceded his book. Stauben's ghetto literature was a response to the revolutionary events in Paris and to a series of violent attacks against Jews in Alsace by a large number of the artisan classes in the region. It connected Jewish and revolutionary values by showing that Alsace, as a region, needed to become part of a nation that includes a variety of different linguistic and cultural customs.

The link with Kompert is clear as Stauben noted a decade after *Letters on Alsatian Manners*, 'the time of the ghetto is past; soon it must only be a poetic memory...the Israelite must become secular, leave off peddling and petty commerce in order to work outdoors'. Following Kompert's Bohemian counterparts and Papal doctrine, Alsatian-Jews were urged to become rural labourers rather than be part of a banking economy. In this way Jews could establish themselves securely as redeemed French men and women. Such socializing precepts began in counter-reformation Rome and ended, paradoxically, in revolutionary France.

Stauben's fiction portrayed the acceptable face of Jewish particularity—suffering, religiosity, the family, and rural life—characteristics which brought together the French middle classes and its acculturating Jewish minority. Kompert had already made these ethnic and class linkages in a German context. Rather than perceive the ghetto as located far in the past, French and German authors located it on their boundaries. In this way the ghetto impinged directly on the national identity of new Jewish citizens.

The figurative Alsatian ghetto in France was part of a border territory (like Bohemia) and was part of France until the 1871

Franco-Prussian war. It was located within French national boundaries (however insecure) which is why it needed to be integrated and redeemed. The colonial ideal of incorporating the eastern border into the nation-state was, as the novelist W. G. Sebald has argued, a key feature of German ghetto literature which French ghetto literature later reinforced in relation to the Alsace region. As Franzos illustrates, the idea of the 'half-Asian' ghetto on the German eastern frontier fed into widespread anxieties of being overrun from a barbaric territory. The imagined ghetto for both French and German citizens was a place that needed transforming for the new nation-state to become civilized. Modernizers saw the ghetto as an obstacle on the way to progress; pessimists thought it impossible to overcome the orientalizing influence of Jews who had only recently left the ghetto.

Britain

In Britain, Israel Zangwill (1864–1926), the East End of London man of letters, dissident Zionist, and public intellectual, clearly drew on the ghetto literature of Kompert and Franzos. Their work was widely available in English translation by the 1870s and 1880s and proved to be an inspiration for Zangwill's fiction published a decade later. His novel *Children of the Ghetto: A Study of a Peculiar People* (1892) was a sensation and popularized the word 'ghetto' in English. This was the first novel published by the Jewish Publication Society of America (JPSA) and brought together the Jewish 'ghettos' in London and New York, which were both made up of immigrants from Eastern Europe. The novel's subtitle also signalled Zangwill's double vision. It was one part ethnographic ('a study') and one part Dickensian comic grotesque ('a peculiar people').

Zangwill's bestselling novel inspired Abraham Cahan's *Yekl: A Tale of the New York Ghetto* (1896); Herman Heijermans's play *The Ghetto* (1899); Hutchins Hapgood's *The Spirit of the Ghetto* (1902); and David Warfield's *Ghetto Silhouettes* (1902).

These were mainly American stories, plays, and poems (with the exception of the Dutch Heijermans), all of which transplanted Zangwill's 'ghetto' into New York's Lower East Side. The East European immigrants who entered London in the 1880s were part of the same wave of immigration that transformed many of the large northern cities in the United States. By 1914, only New York and Chicago had larger East European 'ghettos' than London.

But it is clear from *Children of the Ghetto* and also Zangwill's stories—*Ghetto Tragedies* (1893), *Dreamers of the Ghetto* (1898), and *Ghetto Comedies* (1907)—that he was steeped in the German tradition of ghetto writing. He both looked back to the works of Kompert and Franzos and looked forward to the 'ghettos' in the urban megacities of New York and Chicago. Zangwill's ethnographic and satirical detachment, his many humanized East European Jewish character types (pedlars, socialists, Zionists, Hebraists, jesters, *schlemiels*) are all reminiscent of the Yiddish-inflected European tradition set in the past. His enlightened critique of religious orthodoxy also chimes with the emancipated outlook of Kompert and Franzos.

As with his predecessors, Zangwill was university-educated but, unlike them, was steeped in the Jewish community as a pupil-teacher in the East End Jewish Free School (JFS) until his early twenties. This double-edged perspective can be found in the 'Proem' to *Children of the Ghetto* which positions the 'London ghetto' somewhere between Italian ghettos and the present day:

> Not here in our London Ghetto the gates and gabardines of the olden Ghetto of the Eternal City; yet no signs of external by which one may know it, and those who dwell therein. Its narrow streets have no speciality of architecture; its dirt is not picturesque. It is no longer the stage for the high-buskined tragedy of massacre and martyrdom; only for the obscurer, deeper tragedy that evolves from the pressure of its own inward forces, and the long-drawn-out tragi-comedy of sordid and shifty poverty.

Although the London ghetto is not walled and gated like Rome (which was extant in living memory) it is made up of 'narrow streets'—the title of one of Kompert's last collections of stories—a name given to medieval Jewish quarters and the Frankfurt *Judengasse*. At the same time, the London ghetto eschews the grandeur of history ('massacre and martyrdom') and even the poetry of past ghettos ('its dirt is not picturesque'). Instead, the 'raw air of English reality' reveals a more mundane world ('sordid and shifty poverty'). Zangwill's ghetto is a 'human palimpsest' which layers multiple ghetto histories and memories onto the present-day 'ghetto'.

Children of the Ghetto was commissioned by the JPSA to humanize the mass immigration from Eastern Europe. It was said to have delayed by a decade the implementation of Britain's first anti-immigration act of 1905. Zangwill could command audiences of 3,000 on his British lecture tour to promote the novel, and so was certainly influential. Referring back to earlier 19th-century stories and novels, Zangwill was at pains to demonstrate that ghetto-dwellers were potentially good citizens. He did this in two main ways. First, he showed that ghetto life was similar to other forms of urban life by focusing on a series of institutions—soup kitchens, trade unions, sweatshops, the Holy Land League, Jewish schools, newspapers, synagogues large and small—all dominated by egotistical and incompetent men.

It was these institutional chapters, set in one of the most densely populated districts in Europe, which earned Zangwill the sobriquet the 'Jewish Charles Dickens'. The 'raw air of [Dickensian] English reality' swept through much of the first half of the novel which was written in the comic mode. Above all else, Zangwill showed the bungling 'primitive fathers of the Ghetto' at their most harmless. Here the ghetto is no more than a Lilliputian Jewish 'cosmos' next to the might of the British Empire.

But a second set of stories in *Children of the Ghetto* are narrated around two female protagonists, Hannah Jacobs and Esther

Ansell, and tests the paternal boundaries of the ghetto. In this regard, the nearby marketplace makes clear the vitality of the ghetto: 'a pandemonium of caged poultry, clucking and cackling and screaming.... The confectioners' shops...were besieged by hilarious crowds of handsome girls and their young men, fat women and their children'. This is a feminine space where the 'great ladies of the West' throw off the 'veneer of refinement' and the authentic life of the ghetto replaces their appearance of civility.

The contrast here is with the marketplace in Franzos's Barnow stories, which is a site of Jewish degeneracy where 'confusion reigns supreme' and where people 'howl' like the 'wretched inmates of bedlam'. Zangwill's marketplace is on the side of life and vitality and connects people of all classes and genders. It is the opposite of a closed-off 'bedlam'.

The plots of Hannah Jacobs and Esther Ansell reinforce the 'nostalgia of the Ghetto' which goes back to Kompert. Jacobs is tempted to elope with her secular Jewish lover but chooses instead to remain in the ghetto with her rabbinical father. Ansell, in a similar plot line, initially moves back to the ghetto from the suburbs. Both heroines replicate the return narratives of Kompert and the nostalgic appeal of the spiritual and life-affirming values of the ghetto. Ansell eventually rejects her lover's marriage proposal on the grounds that it is unwise to 'wed with the grey spirit of the Ghetto that doubts itself'. The 'grey spirit' of the ghetto is dull and masculine. Instead, she takes her 'hopes and dreams across the great water to the New World' emulating Zangwill's later belief in the United States as a redemptive 'melting-pot'.

Zangwill did not follow Kompert and Franzos in calling for the assimilation (that is, Anglicization or Germanization) of ghetto Jews and, instead, he moved in the direction of Jewish nationalism and cultural pluralism. He was against the 'respectability' of upwardly mobile Jews which froze the 'blood of the orient' into the 'uniform grey of English middle-class life'. This belief was dramatized most fully in *Grandchildren of the Ghetto*, the novel which followed *Children of the Ghetto*. Such acculturation lacked the 'full alfresco flavour' of the traditional ghetto. The 'voluntary' ghetto may be peopled by those who carry their 'own Ghetto gates' around with them. But, as both Hannah Jacobs and Esther Ansell show, the ghetto could also be expansive and on the side of broad national and international perspectives.

In an early essay called 'The Ghetto' (1897), Zangwill directly followed Kompert and stressed that the ghetto is a 'realm of poetry, almost a dream world', which demonstrates that the 'Jew's *only* value to the world, his justification for his persistence, is his spiritual originality'. For Zangwill, it is the 'development on modern lines' of the 'spirituality and heroism of the ghetto that [can bring about] the physical salvation for the Jew' or, at least, the 'dignified continuation of Jewish life'. Here Zangwill anticipates Max Nordau's speech to the First Zionist Congress where Nordau, Zangwill's lifelong friend, evoked 'the ghetto' as containing 'specifically Jewish qualities that were esteemed' and were 'the greatest spur to the human spirit'. Far from preventing Jews from becoming good citizens, the ghetto, as a site of communal spirituality, was able to utilize Jewish national values for all humanity.

America

The English translations of Kompert's *Scenes from the Ghetto* and Franzos's *The Jews of Barnow* were reviewed in the *New York Times* in 1882. Within a decade, the word 'ghetto' was commonplace in the United States which was soon reinforced by Zangwill's *Children of the Ghetto*. The early 1880s was the start of mass Eastern European immigration into Staten Island after hundreds of pogroms in the Russian Empire beginning in 1881. By the 1890s, 200,000 Jewish immigrants entered the United States. Three decades later there were close to two and a half

5. New York's Lower East Side.

million East European Jewish immigrants in America before the introduction of stringent anti-immigration legislation in 1924. The vast majority of newly arrived immigrants lived in the Lower East Side of New York (half a million; see Figure 5) and in other north-eastern cities such as Chicago's 'Great West Side' (quarter of a million). These areas were soon known as 'ghettos' or 'Jewtowns'.

The writer and editor Abraham Cahan (1860–1951), an early immigrant from Russia and self-styled 'Friend of the Ghetto', was to become the main spokesperson for these East European immigrants. Cahan arrived in New York in June 1882 and was one of a number of Jewish refugees met by the poet Emma Lazarus (1849–87) in the refugee camp on Ward's Island. At the time, Cahan had no more than a dozen words in English. In contrast, Lazarus, born in New York to a well-to-do family, is best remembered for giving the Statue of Liberty a voice. Her poem 'The New Colossus' (1883) was inspired by witnessing mass immigration:

> Give me your tired, your poor,
> Your huddled masses yearning to breathe free,
> The wretched refuse of your teeming shore.

Within a decade of his arrival, Cahan was writing 'ghetto' stories and, most importantly, was able to transform the Yiddish daily *Forverts* ('Forward') into a powerhouse with an initial readership of 7,500 in 1903 peaking two decades later with 250,000 readers. The acculturated Lazarus, working within a different ghetto tradition, carried a copy of *The Jews of Barnow* when she met Cahan and later wrote two articles on Franzos. Her interest was sparked by an acerbic review of Franzos and Kompert in the *New York Times* and an extraordinarily blinkered introduction to the American edition of *The Jews of Barnow*. The imagined ghettos of Western Europe confronted American realities.

East European refugees tended to settle in ethnic enclaves in the poorest areas of large American cities with the word 'ghetto' soon applied to these areas and picked up by their inhabitants. The American 'ghetto', in other words, exemplified a moribund European history—huddled masses; wretched refuse—which was transported wholesale to the United States. The past was European and needed the New World to transform it.

The *New York Times*, following Franzos, described a newly arrived Jewish woman as a 'forlorn creature' who wears a 'horrible' wig (or *sheitel*). Lazarus countered by noting that together with the 'coarsest weeds…spring the tenderest blossoms of love, piety, and self-sacrifice'. But Lazarus's real dispute (her 'antidote') was in response to the 'poisonous' introduction to the American translation of Franzos's stories by Barnet Phillips. According to Phillips, the Jews of Barnow are 'purely Oriental in character' and reveal 'barbarities even now practiced under sacred religion'.

A founder of the modernizing American Jewish Historical Society, Phillips championed the reformed American-Jew (similar to Franzos championing of the enlightened German-Jew) who overcame age-old 'barbarities' and an oriental character. As Phillips argues: 'It sometimes happens that fiction produces effects where facts fail.... In the hands of the reformed Jew, by means of the lessons it teaches, [he may] save his race from retrogression'. Echoing the Italian ghettos, which were often built next to convents, the ghetto for Phillips was essentially feminine: 'If to live, it must have seclusion, [Judaism in the ghetto] approaches closely to the Eastern idea of a woman's virtue, something wanting the protection of high walls and difficult approaches'. For Barnett the ghetto represents the worst of European history—barbarous, retrogressive, and feminized. Most acculturated German-Jews, who immigrated to New York in the decades before their East European counterparts, agreed with Barnett.

Lazarus, challenging such prejudice, argued that the ghetto is able to 'uplift, to enlighten and to console' its residents and asked her readers to reflect on how strange America must appear from the perspective of the new Russian immigrants. It was this strangeness that Cahan addressed in his fiction. He followed Zangwill in both his realistic and ethnographic depictions of the ghetto and in its sense of communality. That he was primarily a Yiddish writer meant that he, however, differed crucially from Zangwill in his more complex written style. Four years after *Children of the Ghetto*, Cahan published his novella *Yekl: A Tale of the New York Ghetto*. It would have been published sooner in English but many publishers approached in the late 1880s did not know what a 'New York Ghetto' meant.

Cahan began as a journalist, mainly in Yiddish but also in English, and wrote a regular column *Bintel Brief* ('A Bundle of Letters') where, for a quarter of a century, he advised his readers on the intricacies of American acculturation. He was both a socialist and a pragmatist, who had an intimate knowledge of his East European readership and their most pressing concerns. Above all else, he was an intermediary whether it came to strike action, social welfare, or union organization. His fiction (which he mainly wrote in English) reflects this in-between quality not least on the level of language. Zangwill wrote in Dickensian English which did not account for how his Jewish characters actually spoke. Cahan, on the other hand, wrote in a language in transition—from Yiddish to English and back again—which reflected his character's varying levels of integration.

Yekl: A Tale of the New York Ghetto illustrates how complex it was for new immigrants to be part of the ghetto. This was a two-fold process which Cahan traced initially from East European *shtetls* to the New York ghetto and, after acculturation, from the New York ghetto to American society. Cahan's protagonist Jake Podgorny is an anti-hero who disowns his wife left behind in Russia. He, instead, fraternizes in the dance halls with 'the girls' he works with in the sweatshop. When his wife Gitl eventually arrives from her village *shtetl*, after three years, Jake is dismayed by her drab appearance in the modest garb of a devout Jewish woman. She remembers the American Jake as the Russian Yekl. From her perspective Jake/Yekl are two different people.

The novella ends with a twist as Gitl (soon known as Gertie) is advised to arrange a large settlement for her divorce. Jake/Yekl is unsure whether the disavowal of his wife, and his marriage to a 'dancing girl', speaks to his 'heart' or not. Following Kompert, he remains divided between the simplicities of the East European *shtetl* personified by Gitl/Gertie and the forceful energies of the New York ghetto:

> The East Side…became the Ghetto of the American metropolis, and, indeed, the metropolis of the ghettos of the world. It is one of the most densely populated spots on the face of the earth—a seething human sea fed by streams, streamlets, and rills of immigration flowing from all the Yiddish-speaking centres of Europe.

Not unlike Zangwill's novels, Cahan's fiction demystifies the ghetto and makes it comprehensible. Cahan had heard Zangwill speak in New York as a 'realist' novelist on several occasions. As a 'Russian realist' himself, Cahan was promoted by the influential Willian Dean Howells who was known humorously as 'The Dean of American Letters'. The dramatic version of *Children of the Ghetto* was first shown on Broadway in 1899 and also influenced Cahan who portrayed the New York ghetto along the lines of Zangwill's didacticism. This influence was made explicit when Cahan helped Hutchins Hapgood write *The Spirit of the Ghetto* (1902). Hapgood was a Harvard-educated journalist who worked with Cahan on the *New York Commercial Advertiser*. His book was a largely sympathetic journalistic account of the Lower East Side which saw the ghetto as a site of spirituality.

Hapgood stated in his preface that the New York ghetto was not a place of 'poverty, dirt, ignorance and immorality' but, rather, full of 'charm'. His benevolent portrayal was in direct response to Jacob Riis's book, *How the Other Half Lives: Studies among the Tenements of New York* (1890). Riis, writing in the anti-ghetto tradition of Franzos and Barnett, characterized 'Jewtown' (as he called it) as a place where 'Typhus and small-pox are bred' and where 'only the demands of religious custom has the power to make [Jewish] parents clean up at stated intervals'. Such is the spiritual ghetto, which could aid the whole of humanity, and the ghetto as a place of dirt and disease which needed to be demolished. These bitter-sweet versions of the ghetto, a commonplace in European conventions, had come home to America.

By World War I, a new generation of ghetto writers had begun to lay the foundations of Jewish-American literature. Cahan's *The Rise of David Levinsky* (1917) was published at the same time as the memoirs and fiction of Mary Antin (1881–1949) and Anzia Yezierska (1880–1970). This mainly first-person 'ghetto' literature culminated with Henry Roth's novelistic masterpiece *Call it Sleep* (1934). But, as Wayne Miller shows in his anthology, *A Gathering*

of Ghetto Writers: Irish, Italian, Jewish, Black, Puerto Rican
(1972) there was a wide range of pre-war American 'ghetto writers'
in the first half of the 20th century.

By the 1930s, standard American dictionaries defined the 'ghetto'
as 'any section of a city or town inhabited chiefly by members of a
minority group'. At the same time, it was soon recognized that a
crucial distinction needed to be made between 'European
immigrant experiences in ethnic clusters' and those of black
Americans: 'The Jews' ghetto, unlike the Negroes' was a gateway.
It served to help them get in [to America] rather than keep them
locked out'. With this crucial difference in mind, the European
ghetto finally became Americanized. Even with the variety of
'ghetto writers' in his collection, Miller concludes that, 'for most
Americans "ghetto" and "black" are practically synonymous'. This
transition from Europe to the United States, and from Jewish to
black history, began as early as the 1920s and characterized the
American national imaginary by the 1960s.

Chapter 4
Nazism and the ghetto

One of the most moving histories of the Rome-Jewish community, the oldest diaspora Jewish community, was published in 1940. The author of the book, Herman Vogelstein (1870–1942), escaped from Poland to England in 1938 and travelled to the United States in 1939. He spent the last few years of his life ensuring that his short book on Rome (based on a longer German-language version) was published in English. Vogelstein apologized in his preface for the lack of any up-to-date research (impeded by the fascist government in Italy) and for the dearth of scholarly references ('my library and all my writings are lost'). In exile, without his library, his book recreated a world recently destroyed.

Although the ancient Rome-Jewish community lasted for nearly two millennia, a third of Vogelstein's history is concerned with the Rome ghetto (1555–1870). The analogy between the ghettos of the early modern past and those of the present was not uncommon after the 1935 Nuremberg Racial Purity Laws. These laws for the 'Protection of German Blood and Honour' stripped German-Jews of their citizenship and made sexual relations with 'Aryans' illegal. They also instituted a boycott of 'Jewish businesses' and prevented Jews from entering the major professions and the civil service. Such ostracism and inevitable impoverishment reinforced the idea among many German-Jews that they were once again living in a 'ghetto'.

For around half a million German-Jews, the Nuremberg Laws were devastating and inexplicable. They needed a new vocabulary to understand such an unprecedented act of state-sponsored racial exclusion. Without this vocabulary many German-Jews thought of themselves as returning to a 'medieval ghetto' as part of a continuous history of Jewish suffering. While such timeless persecution was one explanation for their segregation and social isolation, there were those, with a greater historical understanding, who did not confuse the medieval ghetto with the rise of Nazism. Joachim Prinz, a young Berlin-based liberal rabbi, gave a sermon in 1935 in response to Hitler's assumption of power two years earlier. A few months before the Nuremberg Laws, Prinz was at pains to illustrate the difference between the historic age of the ghetto and present-day Nazism:

> The medieval ghetto was sealed at night.... The bolt was thrown deliberately: one left the 'world' and entered the ghetto. Today the situation is just the opposite. When the door of our houses closes behind us, *we leave the ghetto and enter our homes.* This is the basic difference. The ghetto is no longer a geographical area, at least not in the sense of the Middle Ages. The ghetto is the 'world'.

Prinz characterized the 'true name' of this form of isolation—'*The Jewish destiny is to have no neighbour*'—as 'Ghetto 1935'. The Italian ghettos encouraged a qualified means of integration into early modern city-states, whereas 'Ghetto 1935' with its 'invisible walls' was a form of internal expulsion: 'In the markets, in the street, in the hotels…in every place'. Prinz was fortunate enough to be able to travel to the United States in 1937. His previous world, after the lull of the 1936 Berlin Olympics, had turned into a ghetto.

German literature transformed the setting of the figurative ghetto from Western to Eastern Europe. This act of imaginative remapping was reinforced by Nazi ideologists who assumed that the ghetto was indigenous to Eastern Europe. As Yiddish and

German are closely related languages it is not surprising that Yiddish writers eventually used the German word 'getto' instead of the indigenous *shtetl*. As the historian Daniel B. Schwartz has shown, Yiddish authors in exile debated, rather too abstractly, whether it made sense to 'return to the ghetto' or not.

'Ghetto 1935' was an 'invisible ghetto' in Germany. Enforced Jewish social isolation, and economic exploitation and evisceration, were preferred by policymakers to the recreation of walled enclaves. The German authorities, who strictly monitored the Jewish community, noted the increased use of 'ghetto' in lectures and journals after the Nuremberg Laws. This proved to be a useful propaganda tool. By returning Jews to the ghetto, with the same compulsory yellow markings eventually introduced, it was as if the Germans were merely reverting back to less troubling times. Written in the mid-1930s, a Hitler Youth leaflet read: 'As a member of an alien race, the Jew in the Middle Ages had no rights of citizenship. He had to live in a separate quarter, the ghetto'.

But there were no ghettos in Western Europe (including Germany). A version of the Nuremberg Laws was extended to Western European nations under German control to monitor, deplete, and isolate Jews before deportation. Most German policymakers were actively against the establishment of fixed ghettos as they thought that a collective Jewish presence was potentially infectious. They were also aware that many Jewish nationalists welcomed the ghetto as a form of collective empowerment. Although ghettoization was discussed in relation to some Western European cities, especially Amsterdam, the policy was not carried out. One suggestion was to relocate Jews into a 'special neighbourhood' on the outskirts of Berlin where they would live in small 'Jewish houses' (*Judenhäuser*). But, while impoverished Jews were forced to move to 'Jewish houses', the idea of permanent Jewish dwellings in Berlin were abhorrent to most German policymakers. The extent to which such ideas where anathema can be seen in the comments of Reinhard Heydrich, Chief of Police and the Gestapo, in November 1938:

> From a police point of view a ghetto, in the form of a completely segregated district with only Jews, is not possible. We would have no control over a ghetto where the Jew gets together with the whole of his Jewish tribe. It would be a permanent hideout for criminals and first of all a source of epidemics and the like.

This statement was made in the office of the deputy Führer, Hermann Göring, two days after *Kristallnacht* or the 'night of broken glass'. This was an organized bout of violence (with 30,000 Jews incarcerated) and nearly all Jewish communal institutions in Germany, Austria, Bohemia, and Moravia destroyed. Whether there should be a policy of 'ghettoization', in response to *Kristallnacht*, was part of a wider discussion concerning the so-called 'Jewish Problem' which took place at the highest levels. In 1938, the preferred 'solution' was to make Jewish lives so intolerable that they would be forced to migrate.

After the invasion of Poland, on 1 September 1939, the question of ghettoization became more acute. The war-time context for this question was crucial as Nazi ideology and military pragmatism were often in conflict. Three and a half million Polish-Jews were trapped in Poland as the Germans expanded eastwards, and, three months after the invasion, the USSR closed its borders. To complicate matters further, Poland was divided into three provinces to enable German continental expansion or *Lebensraum*. In the west, *Warthegau* was annexed to the German Reich and incorporated the Łódź ghetto. Eastern Poland was part of the Soviet Union (under the Nazi-Soviet pact) leaving the General Government (*Generalgouvernement*), the large occupied zone in the middle, under the rule of Hans Frank. Krakow was made its capital and Frank incorporated the largest of all the ghettos, the Warsaw ghetto, into his domain.

The *Warthegau* aimed to denude its region of Poles, Roma, and Jews and repopulate the Reich with around one and a half million 'ethnic Germans' (*Volksdeutsche*). But it was in the region of the General Government that the vast majority of Jews (four times greater than in Germany) were encountered. Many of these East European Jews (*Ostjuden*) wore religious garb and conformed to the Nazi racial imaginary concerning the vermin-like 'ghetto Jew'. Such race-thinking associated bearded, kaftan-wearing Jews with an overcrowded 'Asian' ghetto that was above all a 'plague' source or a 'colony of filth'. The Nazi ghetto was now firmly located in the East and was filled with subhuman *Ostjuden*.

Soon after the invasion, Heydrich distributed a *Schnellbrief* (an express letter) to the leaders of the *Einsatzgruppen* (mobile death squads) who were deployed in Poland under his command. Early histories of the Holocaust have argued that this letter was a centralized plan to ghettoize Jews and Roma as a prelude to the subsequent genocide. After all, Heydrich did speak of the 'final aim (which will require extended periods of time)' and stated that:

> Jewry in the cities should be contained in the ghetto [*im getto*], to permit better control and, subsequently, their better removal. Along with this, it is urgent that the Jew as smallholder disappear from the rural regions. This operation must be accomplished within the next three to four weeks.

But the 'final aim' was a vague aspiration in 1939 and, in the short timescale ('three to four weeks'), was impossible to carry out. Most relevantly, Heydrich used the phrase *im getto* meaning 'in the ghetto' which, as the historian Dan Michman notes astutely, referred to extant Jewish townships or *shtetls*. Most historians now agree that this was not a general policy of ghettoization—or the creation of ghettos with a view to the Final Solution—but a pragmatic means of enclosing Jews in their existing urban neighbourhoods.

The vitality of Jewish cultural life in the larger Polish ghettos reinforced a sense that this was merely a continued form of centuries-old self-government rather than genocide. Larger ghettos, unlike concentration camps, often included secret chroniclers, makeshift theatres, rough concert venues, and a wide variety of political groupings. Ghetto-dwellers could even imagine a continuity of Jewish traditions as if the Yiddish-speaking policemen had come from Tel Aviv (as one occupant put it). Heydrich in the *Schnellbrief* insisted that each ghetto has twenty-four 'Jewish Elders' making up *Judenräte* or 'Jewish councils'. There were forms of *Judenräte* without ghettos which also negotiated with the Nazi authorities. But such councils were nothing like the traditional *Kehilla* in Eastern Europe which ran Jewish communities. *Judenräte* were a German creation and were, according to Heydrich, 'fully responsible' (in the literal sense) for carrying out German directives. They were an essential means for 'soliciting the co-operation of the victims', in Zygmunt Bauman's telling phrase as both sociologist and survivor, which is merely an illusion of autonomy.

Łódź ghetto (1940–4)

The foremost industrial city of Łódź, a major centre of textile production, was located in the *Warthegau* zone of the expanded German Reich. Before the war nearly a third of its population, around 230,000 people, were born Jewish and had lived there for nearly 150 years. Given that the racial vision of Nazism was to 'Aryanize' the expanded Reich the creation of a ghetto in Łódź was particularly unpopular among the local German rulers. 'Aryanization' or racial purification could only be achieved with mass deportations to Lublin and Nisko in Eastern Poland (favoured by Adolf Eichmann) to create a 'reservation' or *Reichsghetto*. Later the fantasy of deporting Jews to the Island of Madagascar or the Soviet Gulag was thought of as a means of creating a *judenrein* (or Jew-free) Poland. But such a vast population transfer was unattainable in the early months of the war.

Friedrich Übelhör, responsible for establishing a 'closed ghetto' in Łódź in December 1939, made it clear that this was to be a purely interim undertaking as 300,000 Jews had already fled eastward into the Soviet zone with another 400,000 trapped in the *Warthegau*:

> The establishment of the ghetto is of course a transitional measure.
> I reserve to myself the decision concerning the times and the means
> by which the ghetto and with it the city of Łódź will be cleansed of
> Jews. In any event, the final goal must be that we completely burn
> out this plague spot.

But such a ghetto, for an estimated 220,000 Jews in Łódź in January 1940, could not be formed quickly. By the time it was formed, three months later, 57,000 Jews and Roma had escaped either into the countryside where they were nearly all shot or had travelled eastwards where their fate is unknown. There was a delay until the end of April 1940 caused by Übelhör's widespread consultations concerning the boundaries of the ghetto walls, the resettlement of Poles and Germans who already lived there, traffic issues, the control of epidemics, sewage, corpse disposal, food, and heating.

After months of internal discussion, local officials persuaded Übelhör and Arthur Greiser, the Reich Governor of the *Warthegau*, to move all the Jewish residents of Łódź, and surrounding areas, into the slum districts of Baluty and the Old Town where 60,000 Jews already lived. These neglected areas had a high percentage of wooden houses, over a century old, on narrow, unpaved, and unlit alleyways. Both districts were densely populated, prone to typhoid outbreaks, with little or no modern infrastructure (central heating, water, drains, and toilets). Added to the slum districts was suburban Marysin, where the ghetto authorities located themselves and their institutions, and was an enclosed area of 1.6 square miles. Out of a total of 31,000 mainly one-room apartments only 725 had running water. Most did not have electricity but, in any case, lights were forbidden from 8pm to 6am.

From February to March 1940, 100,000 Jews living elsewhere in Łódź were ordered to leave their homes for the squalid ghetto. The relocation passed this deadline and the Germans on the night of 6–7 March ('Bloody Thursday') hauled 200 people from their homes. Three-quarters of them were taken to a nearby woods and shot. The organized pillaging of individual Jews, their institutions, and so-called 'Jewish businesses' had been a regular occurrence since the German occupation. After 'Bloody Thursday', a terrorized population of 163,000 in total was crammed into the ghetto which was sealed off 'hermetically' with fences and barbed wire. Only forty-nine apartments had a bathroom and, on average, each room contained more than three people.

The children in two orphanages were some of the last captive residents to be transferred from the city. By the end of April the ghetto was completely walled in, with just two bridges to the outside, and closed off from the rest of the world. At the same time, the city was renamed Litzmannstadt after the World War I hero, General Karl Litzmann, who was a prominent supporter of Nazism. Litzmannstadt was to become a model German city in the Greater Reich. In this 'Aryan' vision, disease was confined to the ghetto, Jewish wealth was expropriated for the greater good, and the city was to be redeveloped along the lines of a conquering imperial power.

But it was not just the city of Litzmannstadt that was to become a model of its kind. The meticulous planning and supervision that went into the Łódź ghetto was to be studied (often by 'ghetto tourists') as a prototype for other ghettos. After all, the Łódź ghetto was not only the most significant ghetto in the German empire (and the second largest ghetto in former Poland) but it also proved to be extraordinarily productive. It became a 'work ghetto' (as it was called) not by design but in large part because of the appointment of the 62-year-old Chaim Rumkowski as the Elder of the Jews in October 1939.

Rumkowski was a failed businessman who achieved much in the spheres of education and child welfare (which is why he insisted on the orphanages becoming part of the ghetto). Unlike most of his peers, he did not abandon the running of the Jewish community after the Germans invaded. His remit as the 'Elder of the Jews' was far-reaching: 'to carry out all measures of the German civil administration with regard to all persons belonging to the Jewish race'. But his powers were always subordinated to the German authorities. Within weeks of choosing a council of thirty the Germans arrested, imprisoned, or shot all but eight 'elders' to remind Rumkowski of his ultimate subservience.

Rumkowski is extraordinarily controversial. The Auschwitz survivor Primo Levi described him memorably as a dictatorial figure who 'adopted the oratorical technique of Mussolini and Hitler...the creation of consent through subjugation and plaudit'. But, as Levi recognized, these are not black and white issues. Rumkowski occupied an ethical 'grey zone' in using his dictatorial powers (reinforced by ghetto and German police) to create a skilled workforce. They ended up making *Wehrmacht* uniforms and equipment as well as clothes for the German civilian market. The transformation of a slum area, with the minimum of infrastructure, into a significant element of the German economy was no mean achievement (see Figure 6).

According to their race-thinking, the Germans assumed that there was untold wealth in the ghetto to pay around 3,000 maintenance workers. The German and Jewish police, located within the ghetto, ransacked each living quarter to discover these mythical riches. They even withheld food supplies for two weeks to compel the treasure to appear. But, in reality, Rumkowski had to find a means of running the ghetto—to buy medicine, food, fuel, and raw materials—and requested a budget to put 8,000–10,000 skilled

6. Łódź ghetto workforce.

artisans to work. The authorities were asked to supply raw materials and pay the poverty wages of the labourers. But this needed a completely different perspective from the German authorities. Rather than extracting hidden wealth from 'the Jews', the ghetto would create income, paid in food supplies, through its workforce.

Soon after the ghetto was sealed off, the first textile workshop was operating and, by September, there were seventeen. But, without modern machinery, the work was slow and unskilled. The arrival of Hans Biebow, who ran the Food and Economy Office of the German ghetto administration, changed matters considerably. The link between productive work and extra food for labourers became an established fact as Biebow, Greiser, and their underlings made huge profits from this arrangement. Soon Biebow had an office of 400 staff and the Łódź ghetto became a 'work ghetto' *par excellence*. The ghetto was no longer transitional but, instead, was established as a permanent fixture with modern machinery which needed servicing.

This was not, however, a settled matter. Biebow's deputy, Alexander Palfinger, argued against the idea of a self-sustained ghetto as it was anathema to his racial notions of purification. As with many other high-ranking Nazi officials, Palfinger preferred the attritional view of ghettoization: 'The rapid dying out of the Jews is a matter of total indifference'. Given that most Jews in the ghetto were on starvation diets of 800 calories daily, extra rations in exchange for labour would merely prolong their lives unnecessarily. But the reality of a small city of Jews on the outskirts of Litzmannstadt had to be faced to avoid it being turned into a necropolis. The Łódź ghetto was a local problem which needed local solutions.

Harsh factory conditions, with twelve-hour days and impossibly high quotas, resulted in several strikes as the ghetto was made up of a variety of workers' organizations (both socialist and Zionist). The death rate increased, from 1940 onwards, to more than 1,000 a month and, by 1942, it had reached 2,000 a month. The economics of the ghetto was always precarious as the Germans paid the bare minimum for merchandise and insisted on the highest possible taxation. If food ingredients were available, there was hardly any fuel (especially coal) to heat them which meant that soup kitchens, designed for welfare cases, could not operate. The result was a workforce that, at its lowest point, had nothing more than potato peelings (used for horse fodder) to sustain them.

The success, of the Łódź ghetto as a 'work ghetto' (in Biebow's formulation) was, to say the least, double-edged. Only 'productive' labourers survived as the rest of the ghetto was deemed to be made up of 'useless eaters'. Women, children, the elderly—as well as teachers, hospital staff, criminals, and those who worked in the old age home, prayer houses, or orphanages—were 'dispensable'. Those earmarked for deportation had to plead with the *Judenrat* for their, or their families', continued existence in the ghetto.

All sixty ghettos in the *Warthegau* were liquidated by the early months of 1943 with 20,000 'productive' labourers transferred to Łódź and thousands of others interred in slave labour camps. Most ghettos, not least the Warsaw ghetto, were divided into those who were employable and those who were unemployable. By 1942, it was clear that 'non-productive' meant a death sentence at Chełmno located just over 30 miles north-west of Łódź.

Chełmno was an experimental death camp which, from 8 December 1941, used gas to kill around 300,000 Jews and Roma from all over Poland. Before his assassination in June 1942, Heydrich authorized the murder of 100,000 Jews in the *Warthegau* in the first half of 1942. The order was given just after the Wannsee Conference which radicalized mass murder so that it became a policy of genocide. By this time, Łódź was regarded as a regional ghetto. As a result, at the end of 1942, 20,000 mainly West European Jews were transported to Łódź from, among other major cities, Berlin, Vienna, Prague, and Frankfurt putting enormous pressure on the ghetto's resources. Five thousand Roma (out of 30,000 in Poland) also entered the ghetto at this time.

To make room for these Roma and 'westerners' (as they were known), Rumkowski was told to deport those in the ghetto who were not employed in the workshops. From December 1941 to May 1942, 57,000 people were deported. At first Rumkowski claimed not to know their destination but, when their goods and clothes came back to the ghetto for sorting, it was clear that they were being murdered at Chełmno. Four months later, at the start of September 1942, 11,000 sick and elderly and 9,000 children under the age of 10 were sent to Chełmno. In one of his many set piece speeches—'Give Me Your Children'—Rumkowski maintained that he had to 'cut off limbs in order to save the body itself' and that he needed 'your children' handed over 'so that we can avoid further victims'.

Rumkowski arranged for a gigantic banner in the ghetto which read 'Work Is Our Only Path'. He imagined himself in the role of

Noah protecting his people from the flood in the ark of the ghetto. But work was not the only path and he could not protect his 'children' or anyone else from the death camps beyond his domain. There were many who were not able to contribute to the workshops. Middle-class 'westerners' committed suicide in high numbers and often chose deportation to life in the ghetto. The Roma, who were immediately thought of as troublemakers, were also sent speedily to their deaths. It was Operation Reinhard (1941–3), which marked the assassination of Reinhard Heydrich, that gave the lie to Rumkowski's work ethos. The operation replaced the policy of mass expulsion from Poland with that of mass extermination and resulted in the death of 1.2 million Jews in the newly built extermination camps Chełmno, Treblinka, Sobibor, and Belzec. The Łódź ghetto could not possibly avoid such an onslaught.

By 1943, Łódź was a labour camp of around 70,000 specialized workers with 117 factory workshops. They made an extraordinarily wide variety of merchandise including military and civilian clothes, and accessories for both men and women. It was undoubtedly a cash cow for Greiser and Biebow who argued vociferously with the Berlin authorities that it should continue to produce goods for the German economy. This line of argument was accepted throughout 1943 where the focus was almost entirely on the production of goods with close to full employment for the 75,000 workers. There was only one small deportation in March of that year. By September 1944, despite the support of Albert Speer, the armaments minister, the ghetto was earmarked for liquidation and its population evacuated to Auschwitz-Birkenau. It was the last ghetto standing on Polish soil but was never going to be the exception to the Final Solution.

Many of those who wrote a daily chronicle in Łódź were deeply critical of Rumkowski and his messiah complex, although such criticisms were reserved for private diaries. Rumkowski believed that the ghetto could outlast the war and that he would be able to lead out his 'golden' workforce in triumph. It was not an entirely deluded hope as there was only a three-month gap between the destruction of the ghetto and Soviet troops entering Łódź. No one quite knows what happened to Rumkowski except that he and his extended family ended up in the crematoria at Birkenau. Biebow generally did not care at all about the lives of those in the ghetto and organized its liquidation. But he is said to have arranged a special car for Rumkowski and his family at the end of the Auschwitz-Birkenau convey. He also wrote a letter to the Camp Kommandant on behalf of the erstwhile 'King of the Jews' (as Rumkowski was known) but to no avail.

Rumkowski's dictatorial control of the ghetto had two main negative consequences. Unlike most other ghettos, there was no black market with food smuggled in from the outside which meant that the starvation diets within the ghetto were entirely at the whim of the Germans. Łódź had its own currency to prevent smuggling or a 'black economy' and its borders were more tightly policed than any other ghetto. The lack of smuggled food resulted in the highest death rate of any large ghetto.

When the ghetto was finally destined for liquidation, with around 70,000 people understanding that this was a death sentence, there was little capacity for resistance. Rumkowski had long since crushed any political opposition and any possibility of firearms or an autonomous Jewish militia. The Jewish police were his personal militia and ensured that there was no alternative to the 'King of the Jews'. In this, and in many other ways, the Łódź ghetto differed greatly from the Warsaw ghetto built in its wake.

Warsaw ghetto (1940–3)

The Warsaw ghetto was both the largest ghetto in occupied Poland (with, at its peak, 460,000 captive inhabitants) and also the largest European ghetto of any era. Before the German invasion Warsaw was the political and cultural centre of Jewish life in

Eastern Europe. The Polish army heroically resisted the German invasion for twenty days until the end of September 1939 but a quarter of the city's buildings were destroyed or damaged by the air bombardment. Before the establishment of the ghetto, the Germans conscripted 100,000 slave labourers (over a quarter of the Jewish population). This was a brutal short-term measure as the largest of all ghettos was delayed for nearly a year with the minimum of centralized planning. Ghetto formation was not a predetermined element of the Final Solution as the long delay in Warsaw illustrates. Apart from Heydrich's *Schnellbrief*, there were few if any directives from Berlin which would have made this a priority.

Nearly a third of all Polish Jews under German control were located in the Warsaw and Łódź ghettos. But the Warsaw ghetto was ruled from the new capital city Kraków by the General Governor Hans Frank. Unlike the meticulously planned Łódź ghetto, there were many unresolved debates and false starts between Kraków and Warsaw. None of the parameters of the ghetto—its boundaries, its purpose, its population, its longevity—were certain. The key dispute, as the historian Christopher Browning has shown, was between those who wanted to emulate Łódź as a 'work ghetto' and those who believed that the ghetto should be attritional, leaving its supposedly diseased population to starve to death. Such wrangling between the ideological purists (who thought of Jews as no more than rabid 'animals') and the pragmatists (who recognized the need for labour) was one key reason why it took until November 1940 before the ghetto was finally sealed.

The other main reason was that Warsaw, badly damaged and lacking basic amenities, was twice the size of Łódź. Before the invasion, the Jewish population of over 350,000 was a third larger than Łódź's and, over the next few months, was compelled to include the residents of nearby towns. When the ghetto was finally separated from the rest of Warsaw it covered 452 acres and was surrounded by 11 miles of roughly built wall (leaving plenty of gaps for smugglers). Thirty per cent of Warsaw's population were jammed into 2.5 per cent of the city which included the northern outskirts where Jews lived traditionally. The population transfers needed to form the ghetto were immense, with 138,000 Jews forced to leave their homes and 113,000 Poles obliged to move out of their residencies. Even with severe overcrowding, the ghetto after being sealed was to increase its population size by 100,000 in four months.

For all his many faults, Rumkowski set out to create an equal society in the Łódź ghetto by regulating income and food rationing (for those who worked) and providing welfare services (for those who were not working). When he visited the Warsaw ghetto he was appalled that the 'elder' of the *Judenrat*, Adam Czerniaków, presided over a laissez-faire ghetto which led to extremes of wealth and poverty and high rates of mortality. In 1941, 43,000 people died in the ghetto (many due to a typhus epidemic) which was 10 per cent of its overall population. To his disdain, Rumkowski witnessed many hundreds starving in the streets with bodies piled up waiting to be buried. Close to these areas were cafés and a few plush restaurants for the tiny number of ghetto residents, such as professional smugglers, who could dress and spend conspicuously.

The decentralized structure of the Warsaw ghetto meant that the *Judenrat* was not the only source of power and authority. There were German, Polish, and Jewish police formed to patrol the boundaries with the final two susceptible to bribery. Alternative sources of authority varied from different political groups organizing welfare for their members to factories exporting goods outside of the official German economy. The underground black economy, fuelled by both individuals and groups of smugglers, created alternative forms of food and goods to be bartered or purchased. Children, in particular, were adept at finding small fissures in the surrounding walls and made up the majority of individual smugglers. Poems and many pieces of reportage were dedicated to the life-saving child-smugglers. Some German policemen even enabled children to cross in and out of the ghetto.

With the official daily ration of fewer than 200 calories, designed to starve the populace, it was estimated that 80 per cent of food in the ghetto was trafficked from outside. This estimate was based on a study by *Oyneg Shabbos* ('Sabbath Delight'), a group of sixty writers, doctors, teachers, and eyewitnesses in the ghetto hand-picked by Emmanuel Ringelblum. Unlike the daily chroniclers of the Łódź ghetto, who were authorized by Rumkowski, the clandestine *Oyneg Shabbos* actively opposed the *Judenrat* and was connected to the underground resistance. Ringelblum wrote a doctorate on the history of Warsaw Jewry in the Middle Ages and so understood the differences between historic and contemporary ghettos. He began the archive a month after the ghetto was formed and wanted to 'capture every event of Jewish life in the heat of the moment, when it was fresh and pulsating'.

The day before the ghetto was sealed Chaim Kaplan, a member of *Oyneg Shabbos*, wrote that 'we went to bed in the Jewish quarter, and the next moment we woke up in a closed ghetto'. The Nazi ghetto was something entirely unprecedented, and Ringelblum was at pains to collect as much evidence as possible, from a victim's perspective, about this new situation. The *Oyneg Shabbos* group, with some outside funding, was able to collect diaries, letters, details of cultural events, school reports, official documents of all kinds, and notes from Allied radio.

It also engaged in two kinds of underground research. One concerned the experience of those in the ghetto (economically, physiologically, politically) and the other collected rare eyewitness accounts of the death camps and the destruction of nearby towns and villages. Key reports were passed on to Polish and Jewish partisans with some of these reports reaching the London-based Polish government in exile. Ringelblum recognized his own work on hearing a British broadcast on the horrors of Chełmno in the summer of 1942: 'we have revealed [Hitler's] satanic plan to annihilate Polish Jewry, a plan which he meant to complete in silence'. But the Allies did not act on the knowledge provided by an eyewitness who had been forced to dig 'mass graves' at Chełmno or the reports of mass starvation in the Warsaw ghetto. Rachel Auerbach, an *Oyneg Shabbos* writer, noted acerbically that the archive had better luck in saving documents than saving people. Including Auerbach, only three out of sixty writers survived the war.

For all the underground activity in the Warsaw ghetto, there was very little resistance to the mass transportations in the second half of 1942. These began in July, six months after the Wannsee Conference, with daily deportations in cattle trucks to the Treblinka extermination camp. Over a quarter of a million Jews were transferred in ten weeks. Another 20,000 were either killed in the ghetto or sent to slave labour camps with 8,000 managing to escape to the 'Aryan' side of Warsaw. While Rumkowski personally supervised the expulsion of orphans in Łódź, to ensure that quotas were met, Janusz Korczak famously volunteered to accompany 190 orphaned children to Treblinka who were under his care. Rumkowski gave a speech saying that he felt desolate at being forced to deport young children whereas Czerniaków, in despair, committed suicide at the height of the savage expulsions. Retaining one's sense of humanity could be deemed to be more important than mere physical survival.

By the end of 1942, in fewer than six months, Treblinka accounted for over 700,000 lives which on average amounted to 4,600 a day or nearly 200 an hour. This was the fate of 300,000 people deported from the Warsaw ghetto and another 380,000 from as many as sixty smaller ghettos across the General Government. According to the historian David Cesarani the murder of so many people in three gas chambers made Treblinka 'the most lethal place on earth'. Warsaw was officially designated a 'work ghetto' only three months before these mass deportations with thirty factories and nearly 2,000 businesses created. But, after the ghetto was nearly cleared of residents, there were only 36,000 registered workers left to form a slave labour force and, crucially, 20,000 'illegals' remaining in the ghetto. This latter group successfully evaded the ruthless searches around the deportations and eventually formed the core of those who actively resisted the Germans.

In the weeks after the mass transportations there was an unflinching evaluation by Ringelblum: 'Why did Jews not resist when 300,000 of our people were being evacuated from Warsaw? Why was it made so simple and easy for the enemy? Why was there not a single victim among the hangmen?' Most of the ghetto was empty with many abandoned buildings and deserted streets. Such physical destruction anticipated the loss of centuries of Jewish life in Warsaw and Poland as a whole. The reduction of the ghetto to a labour camp (along the Łódź model) happened at the same time as the Jewish Fighting Organisation (known as ŻOB) was created by merging religious and secular, nationalist and socialist organizations. Whereas Łódź was reduced to a conduit for the German economy, there were enough autonomous Jewish political organizations remaining in Warsaw to organize resistance.

The demography of the ghetto changed completely after the ghetto was reduced to fewer than 60,000 inhabitants. Three-quarters of the survivors were aged between 20 and 50, with the majority male, and virtually no children. There was also more food to eat. The Germans, unwittingly, had created the perfect conditions for armed resistance with around 800 activists ready to fight. But the resistance, once formed, had no weapons, no military plans, and their recruits needed basic training. To assert their authority they summarily killed the head of the Jewish police force (who supported the Germans during the mass deportations) and a handful of other high-ranking collaborators. To pay for much-needed weapons, ŻOB collected taxes at gunpoint from the *Judenrat*, factory managers, and anyone else with obvious wealth. The resistance was the de facto ruler of the Warsaw ghetto.

What reinforced the ŻOB as power brokers were rumours of a planned deportation in January 1943 to liquidate the ghetto. The ŻOB built up its arsenal of weapons and confronted the Germans head on. Many of their fighters were killed in these initial encounters but, for the first time, there were around a dozen German fatalities. The leaders of the ŻOB also realized that it was a mistake to face superior firepower (including tanks and artillery) directly. The next day they fought from prepared positions in confined spaces. They had very little option but to fight to the death. Everyone who remained in the ghetto was well aware of the extermination camp which awaited them.

The small-scale German operation lasted only four days as it was planned. But it was immediately celebrated as a successful confrontation which had prevented the Germans from clearing the ghetto. The January Uprising (as it was known) gave 'wings' (as one of its leaders wrote) to the Jewish resistance. After ignoring the ŻOB for many months, the Polish Home Army immediately donated much needed weapons, grenades, and explosives. The youthful Jewish resistance planned meticulously over the next four months how to defend themselves against the military might of the Germans. An extensive network of bunkers and elaborate hiding places were constructed, and armaments were acquired and distributed. These tasks were the main priorities of the ghetto. German workshops were fire-bombed to prevent the transfer of their labourers who subsequently went into hiding. The January Uprising turned out to be a dress rehearsal for the later, and much more significant, Warsaw Ghetto Uprising.

By mid-April, 2,000 well-armed German soldiers and Ukrainian auxiliaries prepared for an assault on the ghetto as if they were going to war. This time the Jewish resistance was well prepared and had received advanced warning of the operation. The 'Aryan' side of Warsaw was to witness, for the first time, elite German troops being rebuffed by a few hundred emaciated Jewish fighters. It was an astonishing sight to see. An army, which had overrun most of the European continent, was being effectively thwarted. In an immediate response to the first few days of fighting, the leaders of ŻOB exchanged letters where they spoke of events having 'surpassed [their] boldest dreams: the Germans ran away from our ghetto twice'. This was the Jewish Stalingrad in miniature.

The Warsaw Ghetto Uprising immediately entered mythology. One member of ŻOB wrote that 'The dream of my life had come true. I've lived to see a Jewish defence of the ghetto in all its greatness and glory'. Most of ŻOB was made up of religious and socialist Zionists which meant that their uprising fed into a national narrative (going back to Biblical times) of Jews fighting a superior power (from Egyptians and Romans to Germans). This biblically inspired narrative replaced the hitherto ubiquitous story of the ghetto as a place of timeless suffering. Even after General von Stropp was called back from the Eastern Front, the ghetto still held out for several more weeks with the ŻOB units forced back into civilian bunkers and, eventually, the sewers. The Germans began to systematically burn down the ghetto, uncovering bunkers, but they were also harassed by ŻOB fighters who remained hidden.

The uprising, which lasted a month, gave succour to the Poles on the outside who, at times, supported the ŻOB and other resistance fighters. The London-based Polish government-in-exile praised the 'courage' and 'determined armed resistance' of the ghetto fighters and called on their compatriots to support them (see Figure 7). Camp victims, such as Jean Améry, who survived Auschwitz-Birkenau, regarded the uprising as an essential means for Jews to regain a sense of their humanity and to escape a 2,000-year-old

7. **The destruction of the Warsaw ghetto after the uprising.**

history of persecution. Jews in Palestine at the time also looked on the ghetto resistance as an exemplar for their own transcendence of diaspora victimhood. That is why the State of Israel has an official commemoration in honour of the ghetto fighters.

The very ubiquity of ghettos throughout Nazi-occupied Eastern Europe has led to the assumption that the policy of ghettoization was uniform and calculated. But the comparison of the two iconic ghettos on Polish soil shows how different they were. The Warsaw ghetto is now regarded as the ghetto of resistance, which has reinforced a narrative of identity formation. Łódź, at the other extreme, for all its Jewish religious and cultural activities, is understood primarily as an extension of the German war economy. One ghetto points in the direction of the continuation of Jewish history; the other to its negation.

Nazi ghettos: from death to display

If we stand back from iconic Warsaw and Łódź, it is possible to gain a sense of the radically different forms of ghettoization in

Poland, the USSR, Hungary, Bohemia, Moravia, and Romania. After the invasion of Soviet-occupied Eastern Europe in 1941, over 1,000 Nazi ghettos had three main geographical locations. Four hundred ghettos were in German-occupied Poland, 500 in eastern Poland, Belarus, Ukraine, and the Baltic States, and around 200 in Central Europe (Hungary, Bohemia, Moravia, and Romania). These ghettos could be open or closed, economic or attritional, concentrated or dispersed; they could last a few weeks or a few years; and they varied in size between a hundred to nearly half a million people.

There were two main factors—timing and location—which determined the type of ghettos built. The timing relates primarily to the summer of 1941 when the Germans reneged on the Nazi-Soviet pact, and invaded eastern Poland, Belarus, Ukraine, and the Baltic States, which were hitherto occupied by the Soviet Union. Operation Barbarossa, as it was known officially, was regarded ideologically as a 'war of extermination' or a means of annihilating 'Judeo-Bolshevism', the Nazi's ultimate enemy. Overcoming this evil combined apocalyptic zeal and military pragmatism, as defeating the Red Army would neutralize the biggest threat to the German domination of the European continent. It was also a means of colonizing much-needed natural resources—oil and farmland—for Germany.

Attacking the Red Army also changed the rules of warfare. The ghettos in the USSR were primarily 'eliminationist' ghettos, as Barbarossa was an extraordinarily bloodthirsty operation resulting in the deaths of nearly two million soldiers in battle. After the Red Army was initially routed in a matter of weeks, 3,000 *Einsatzgruppen* and many more local auxiliaries and German police divisions soon followed to focus on subduing the local Jewish population, partisan activists, and political and religious leaders (often regarded as one and the same). By the summer of 1941, the option of transportations further east or back to Poland was no longer feasible. Transport was needed for the mass mobilization on the Eastern Front, and food, in increasingly short supply, was needed for the military.

Half a million Jews were slaughtered within six months, mainly in trenches and ravines, with a growing number of portable gas vans to speed up the genocide. This mass murder of civilians was in the context of two million Soviet soldiers who were starved to death in prisoner of war camps and one-third of German frontline troops killed after the Red Army stood firm at Stalingrad. The makeshift ghettos, both open and closed but rarely walled in, were a means of isolating a terrified local Jewish population who most often lived within walking distance of their captivity. Many 'remnant ghettos' were divided ominously into two as they included work certificates distributed by the *Judenrat*. They were known colloquially as the 'living' or 'dead' ghettos. All ghettos, and even dispersed communities, had a *Judenrat* and a Jewish police force who, under pain of death, identified Jews in general and those who were 'productive' in particular.

This form of ghettoization (a term only used by the Germans to indicate the construction of individual ghettos) was based on the Polish experience up until 1941 but was paired down savagely and accelerated. Polish ghettos were considered to be holding pens before mass expulsion, whereas the ghettos as part of Operation Barbarossa were part of a policy of genocide. Mass murder often preceded ghettoization or took place a short time after. Soviet ghettos ranged from one street to forty (containing 80,000 in Minsk), and were usually enclosed with barbed wire so that they could be easily reduced in size. The only pause in the slaughter was caused by the ice-cold winter which meant that the ground was too frozen to dig mass graves. All of the nations once occupied by the USSR, and reoccupied by the Germans, broadly conform to this horrific pattern.

Short-term ghettos could be local synagogues, churches, or barns, as well as individual streets, depending on the size of the populace. Larger populations, on pain of death, were confined behind walls (Minsk) or barbed wire (Pinsk, Baranovich), or even on an islet (Słonim). Essential workers were often allowed to leave the ghetto, but there was a general suspicion that Jews were aiding local partisans or were partisans in disguise. Some local rulers did not want to include any form of *Arbeitsjuden* or 'work Jews' and killed the men first, leaving ghettos full of women and children. There were efficient underground groups which enabled hundreds of Jews to escape into the forests further east into the USSR. This was because Jews had more time to prepare resistance further east and were less religiously identifiable under Soviet rule.

The end of the Wannsee Conference in January 1942, chaired by Heydrich, catalysed one of the most murderous years of the Nazi genocide with close to three million Jews killed from March 1942 to February 1943. The mass murders under the guise of Operation Barbarossa were accelerated during this period with another million massacred. By 1943, most towns and cities in German-occupied USSR were without ghettos as the population had been annihilated to save on resources. As a result, there were a few 'working ghettos' or slave labour camps left in each region to aid the war effort. But, when in retreat from the Soviet Army in early 1944, the German's prioritized the destruction of any remaining ghettos or camps. Extermination was placed above labour, even when a quarter of the German workforce in 1944 depended on slave labour.

The German use of the word 'ghetto' carried 'different meanings' in the pursuit of 'different goals' as Michman has shown. In Poland and the USSR false Jewish 'ghettos' were set up by the Germans as a supposed haven from death camps and shooting pits. But they were invariably murder traps. It is a paradox, given the rigidity of Nazi race-thinking, that ghetto was a term with multiple meanings from the late 1930s onwards. This is especially true in the context of Central Europe (Hungary, Bohemia, Moravia) all of which stretched the meaning of 'ghetto'.

Theresienstadt was conceived by Heydrich in late 1941 initially as a transit camp for Czech-Jews so that Bohemia and Moravia could be 'free' of its Jewish presence. It had many characteristics of a concentration camp as it was set up where no Jewish community previously existed in the fortress city of Terezin. The sexes were also separated which resulted in separate women's work details as in the camps. It had a *Judenrat* but a junior branch of the Waffen-SS unusually ran the ghetto directly and eliminated two Jewish 'elders' so that the *Judenrat* remained weak. Theresienstadt was designed uniquely as a place where the most prominent German-Jews—such as war heroes, scientists, and former statesmen—had provided 'special services to the Reich'. Some were protected by high-ranking officials and most were elderly. But the rich educational and cultural life of Theresienstadt meant that it resembled a ghetto in its initial incarnation with 59,000 residents squeezed into around 750 square yards.

The Germans at the time called Theresienstadt by a variety of names—a ghetto for the elderly (*Altersghetto*); a ghetto for distinguished persons (*Prominentenghetto*); the 'city of the Jews' (*Judenstadt*)—just as ghettos in general had multiple designations. But, in the case of Theresienstadt, the ambiguity had a purpose. At the height of the Final Solution in 1943, Theresienstadt began to be 'beautified' and turned into a 'model ghetto' (*Musterghetto*) for propaganda purposes. The benign sense of ghetto (going back to the Middle Ages) was used by the Germans deep into the war. The International Red Cross inspected the ghetto in October 1943 (with Danish delegates) to make sure that the 400 deportees from Denmark were being held in good conditions. Hitler's 'city of the Jews', as it was called, was adequately transformed, with newly painted buildings, cleaned pavements, well-stocked shops, and a sports field.

The hoax worked, not least because 7,500 prisoners were evacuated to create space in the ghetto. But the reality was very different. Out of 155,000 prisoners, who passed through

Theresienstadt, 34,000 perished in the ghetto and 87,000 were sent to death camps. The ghetto turned into a labour camp in its final year, and was the last to be liberated by the Red Army in May 1945 with 29,000 prisoners surviving. The other main 'ghetto' (although that is stretching the term) to be liberated in 1945 was in Budapest.

The 'dispersed ghetto' in Budapest began in April 1944 after the Germans had taken control of Hungary a month earlier. After short-lived ghettoization in over 180 detention centres, 400,000 Hungarian-Jews, in just over three months, were transported to Auschwitz-Birkenau. Budapest-Jews were scheduled to be the last to be deported, and were housed in over 2,000 buildings throughout the city marked with a yellow star. The local authorities objected to a large ghetto for 100,000 Jews as it would have disrupted the running of the city. By July, the Regent of Hungary, Miklós Horthy (who hitherto had cooperated fully with the Germans) ordered that the deportations be suspended.

As the historian Mark Mazower has argued, the 'Jewish Question' was resisted once it moved beyond the borders of Greater Germany and encountered other political authorities. Horthy did create two ghettos in Budapest. A small one for 'foreign Jews' (called the 'international ghetto') and a much larger one for the remaining Jews who were confined to the Jewish districts of Pest. Both ghettos were liberated by the Red Army in January 1945. Created in November and December 1944, the Budapest ghettos, in stark contrast to the rest of Hungary, halted the Nazi genocide. They also reverted back to earlier times—Jewish houses in 1930s Berlin; early Polish ghettos; even Italian ghettos in the case of the 'international ghetto'—which made clear some of the many possible meanings of 'ghetto' even in the context of extermination.

Chapter 5
The ghetto in America

In 1962, James Baldwin, the great African-American novelist, wrote a letter to his nephew about living in 'the ghetto'. He called the letter 'My Dungeon Shook' as it was written in the decade when black youth throughout the decade rose up against their 'imprisoned cities':

> This innocent country set you down in a ghetto in which, in fact, it intended you should perish.... You were born into a society which spelled out with brutal clarity, and in as many ways as possible, that you were a worthless human being. You were not expected to aspire to excellence: you were expected to make peace with mediocrity.

By the 1960s, it was a commonplace to characterize black inner-city slums as 'ghettos' which were understood to have limited the life-chances of those born into them. During this decade, American ghettos—places with 'concentrated poverty' and high rates of 'racial segregation, violence, street crime, joblessness, teenage pregnancy, family instability, school dropouts, welfare receipt, and drug abuse' as the philosopher Tommie Shelby notes—exploded with rage. Those deemed less than human did not just 'shake' the doors of the 'dungeon' but also burnt it down. Beginning with six days of rioting in July 1964 in Harlem, there were over 300 so-called 'race riots' over the next four years. In this period, at a conservative estimate, 52,000 mainly black people were arrested, 220 killed, and 8,000 injured. Baldwin's anger, although considered extreme at the time, was symptomatic.

At the height of the riots, Martin Luther King observed that 'being Negro in America means being herded in ghettos, or reservations, being constantly ignored and made to feel invisible'. Drawing on W. E. B. Du Bois' *Dusk to Dawn* (1940), King described ghetto-dwellers as living 'behind some thick sheet of invisible but horribly tangible plate glass'. Such 'tangible' invisibility was also the subject of Ralph Ellison's fictional masterpiece *Invisible Man* (1952) whose protagonist flees the Harlem ghetto during the 1943 race riots. Ellison was one of the most famous residents of Harlem and one of its most profound observers. He understood the way that the ghetto made black people 'invisible' and isolated them from the rest of the United States. Many scholars have taken up the phrase 'invisible walls' (first used by Joachim Prinz) when trying to understand how the African-American ghetto, at the heart of all the major cities in the north, has become a feature of urban America.

King's reference to being 'herded into ghettos' and to 'invisible walls' that surround ghettos evokes the inhumanity of the Nazi ghettos at a time when American ghettos were considered to be at their most inhumane. Not that there was any consistency about these analogies. At the height of the civil rights campaign, progressive Jews argued that 'we shall provide points of contact between residents and spokesman of the new ghetto and the children and grandchildren of the old ghetto'. But, in speaking of old and new ghettos, Jews for Urban Justice (as they were called), merely reinforced the divide between whitened Jewish-Americans who escaped their 'old ghettos' and African-Americans who remained trapped in urban squalor in 'new ghettos'.

Baldwin, unlike King, highlighted the limitations in evoking Warsaw and Harlem as equivalent ghettos: 'The uprising in the Warsaw Ghetto was not described as a riot, nor were the participants maligned as hoodlums: the boys and girls in Harlem are well aware of this'. For Baldwin 'the Jew is a white man, and when white men rise up against oppression, they are heroes: when black men rise they revert to their native savagery'. To be sure, Baldwin acknowledged that his comparison between Warsaw and Harlem was 'outrageous' as he had ignored the mass deaths in the Warsaw ghetto. But such willed ignorance allowed him to engage with the question of 'race' and racism in the United States. Anti-black racism was the reason why ghettos came into being, why they continued for a century, and why many argue they continue until this day.

The only long-standing ghetto in the United States is the 'Negro' or 'black' or 'African-American' ghetto (depending on the era). These ghettos have been a feature of America's northern cities—at first, Baltimore, Chicago, Cleveland, Detroit, New York, Philadelphia—for more than a century; and Los Angeles and other west coast cities from the 1940s onwards. Such cities were the end point of two Great Black Northern Migrations from the southern states, with New York and Chicago containing the majority of these internal migrants. Around one million mainly rural and unskilled blacks moved into north-eastern cities between 1916 and 1940 and around another five million (many urban labourers) across the whole of the north from 1940 to 1970. Both world wars acted as catalysts for this resettlement (by far the largest internal relocation in the history of the United States) as hundreds of thousands of industrial labourers went overseas to fight, leaving a gap to be filled by the southern newcomers.

Before the Great Migration in 1916, a small number of African-Americans lived in 'Black Belts' (as they were known by non-blacks) in most northern cities. These 'Black Belts' remained a permanent feature of American city-life, in contrast to white ethnic enclaves (1880–1920), whose residents were able to move out of the tenements and urban slums. Before the Great Migration, the relatively small number of 19th- and early

20th-century 'Negroes' in ethnic enclaves were not particularly segregated. To be sure there were patterns of housing and job discrimination but this was akin to the kind of intolerance experienced by new Eastern European, Irish, Italian, Asian, and Hispanic immigrants living in similar 'ethnic enclaves'.

But, unlike these new migrant groups, the forms of discrimination that blacks suffered up until the 1960s were more widespread and organized. This was because the vast majority of 'Negroes' faced restrictive covenants from powerful and deeply hostile Residents Associations from the 1920s to the 1960s which made it virtually impossible for them to move out of the 'Black Belts'. It was during this period that the black 'ghetto' came into being and developed considerably. After the 1916 Great Migration the African-American population in many northern cities grew ten-fold. In 1910, nearly all blacks lived in the south. By the mid-century, two-thirds of African-Americans lived in the north. The response from the white population to this inflow was to create as many impediments as possible (mortgages were unavailable) to prevent southern blacks from moving out of an expanded version of the 'black belt'.

Such enforced living spaces meant that, up until the 1940s, the main point of comparison to black ghettos was the original walled Jewish ghettos in early modern Europe. Short-lived ethnic enclaves no longer served usefully as a point of comparison as they applied to 'white ethnics' only. The early modern Jewish ghettos are more productive as an analogy precisely because they were associated with urban development, modernity, and culture, which, as the African-Americanist Lance Freeman has shown, also applied to the 'Negro ghetto'. During the First Great Migration, the early ghettos were considered a 'promised land' away from slavery, lynching, and segregation. With millions of residents from the rural southern states excluded from the Industrial Revolution, ghettos were on the side of modernization and integration. Many ghettos flourished economically and culturally up until the Great Depression of 1929.

The slump brought hardship and impoverishment to the Negro ghetto as it did to the rest of the United States. But as hardly any blacks could access loans during the best of times they were particularly vulnerable during the worst of times. Roosevelt's New Deal (1933–6) partially alleviated this hardship by funding Public Housing, among other initiatives, for their black residents. In this way ghettos began to be institutionalized both locally and federally with many blacks forced to live in segregated housing projects funded by the state but severely neglected locally. The contrast between the upward mobility of many white Americans (during the boom years of the 1950s) and the economic stagnation in the ghetto 'projects' resulted in some of the most violent disturbances in American history.

The 'ghetto riots' of the 1960s effectively ended the black civil rights era. It was not a coincidence that civil rights legislation was passed at the height of black defiance in the north, reinforcing long-standing protests in the south. All agreed nationally that something had to be done about the 'dark ghetto' (as it was now called) and that such reform was part of black civil rights as King argued. There was a concerted effort to improve black educational and employment opportunities, in response to the civil rights movement, through affirmative action programmes, which resulted in the creation of a significant black middle class. Fair housing legislation enabled better-off black families to relocate away from the poorest areas of the ghetto. This resulted in a gradual but steady suburbanization of the black middle class.

Along with 'white flight' from black urban areas, inner-city ghettos were left ever more destitute and its population completely alienated from society. By the 1980s, theories of a black 'underclass' were popularized by William Julius Wilson, with African-American ghettos seen to house the poorest of the poor. At the turn of the new century, historic ghetto areas were being reclaimed or 'gentrified' by local authorities and commercial property developers. After all, many 'black belts' were first built close to the inner city and prestigious institutions such as universities and banks. By destroying many of the buildings that made up the ghetto in its various incarnations—historic 'black belts' and failed project houses—local mayors could reclaim the inner cities for the wealthy and upwardly mobile. But this policy of gentrification has, to this day, further isolated those who are most in need.

That is why there is still a strong perception by white Americans that deprived black urban areas are, as Bruce Haynes puts it, 'overcrowded communities of filth, starvation, violence and despair'. By focusing on the two largest ghettos in America, New York and Chicago, we will be able to see clearly the different periods of evolution and devolution that are crucial to understanding the complexities of American ghettos. There were periods when ghettos felt free and culturally uplifting, and where black entrepreneurs could flourish. At other times, ghettos felt like prisons, abandoned and overpoliced, with the majority of poor black young men incarcerated and treated as if they were 'worthless' human beings. The key to understanding the American ghetto is as a dynamic phenomenon. Ghettos changed considerably across time and across space and were reconstituted periodically by local and federal authorities. The only thing that does not change is the high percentage of impoverished African-Americans who are still the poorest of the poor.

Chicago

The American ghetto may not have begun in Chicago (New York has that distinction) but studies of the American ghetto certainly did. Louis Wirth's *The Ghetto* (1928) was the first scholarly account of the topic in general and helped found a Chicago School of Urban Sociology. This is not surprising as Chicago, by the 1940s, was the most segregated city in America with 86 per cent of the black population living in areas with a black majority. It was also the second most populated ghetto behind Harlem. Wirth's

The Ghetto is a transitional text beginning with mainly
19th-century versions of the 'medieval' Jewish ghetto and
ending with contemporaneous accounts of the 'Negro Ghetto'
in Chicago's South Side:

> The study of the ghetto is likely to throw light on a number of
> related phenomenon, such as the origin of segregated areas and the
> development of cultural communities in general; for while the
> ghetto is strictly a Jewish institution, there are forms of ghettos that
> concern not merely Jews. There are Little Italys, Little Polands,
> China Towns and Black Belts in our large cities that bear close
> resemblance to the Jewish ghetto.

The Ghetto was important for its scholarly and ethnographic
focus on the urban life of immigrants and minorities. Most
significantly, it encouraged many more ethnographies of the
Negro Ghetto (as it was known) in Chicago. That Wirth's
assumptions were misplaced meant that his pioneering work was
soon qualified by the African-American sociologists that he
mentored at the University of Chicago. His idea that the Black
Belt was 'essentially the same phenomenon that we see in the
social life of other minority groups' made sense before the Great
Migration, but not after.

Wirth's focus on the original area of Jewish settlement in Chicago's
near West Side from the 1870s could not have differed more from
the Black Belt on Chicago's South Side. The Jewish Maxwell Street
Ghetto (as it was known) was the 'first settlement' of tens of
thousands of East European Jews in the Chicago slums. But, by
the time that Wirth was writing his book, there was little left
of the original immigrant community (which he called the
'Vanishing Ghetto') and African-Americans were beginning to
replace the Jewish community. Wirth clearly thought that black
Chicagoans would simply follow immigrant Jews into a less
slum-like 'second settlement'. As the Chicago ethnographers,
St Clair Drake and Horace Clayton asked: 'The Jews had done

it—why couldn't Negroes?' But their *Black Metropolis: A Study of Negro Life in a Northern City* (1945) shows that the experiences of Chicago blacks and Jews were hardly comparable.

Ethnic enclaves, before the Great Migration of 1916, were not the same as 'Negro Ghettos'. Drake and Clayton at first assumed, like Wirth who sponsored their book, that ghettos were 'natural' areas (akin to ecology) where like-minded people would congregate temporarily and gain a certain amount of 'organic' upward mobility. The ultimate goal was assimilation, in the case of Wirth, or integration, in the case of Drake and Clayton. But Wirth, writing in a German-Jewish tradition, had an obvious bias as he thought of ghettos as a preliminary form of settlement preparing immigrants and minorities for full citizenship. As Drake and Clayton were to recognize, this model of natural development did not apply to the Black Belt.

World War I began to restrict immigration into the United States. The war also drew on many workers for the army while creating a vast demand for war-time industrial labour. It was in this context that the Great Migration from the southern states was encouraged in 1916. After migration, Chicago's black population rose to 110,000 in 1920 (from 40,000 in 1910) and grew to 278,000 in 1940. An astonishingly high number of southern newcomers travelled to Chicago as it was a major industrial city and the hub of America's railway network. Wirth missed this crucial background. The massive increase in the southern-born black population did not move on but were forced to stay within the narrow confines of the Black Belt.

The Black Belt was shaped like an isosceles triangle. It stretched thirty blocks along State Street on the South Side and was rarely more than seven blocks or a quarter of a mile wide. The point of the triangle was in the north where the bus and train stations were based, near a slum district which was the historic end of the Black Belt. Two sides of the triangle extended southwards for nearly 15 miles with more upmarket properties at the southern end. Along with innumerable churches of every denomination, this district included many shopping areas, department stores, banks, nightclubs, film theatres, and many iconic black institutions such as the Regal Theatre, Savoy Ballroom, and Hotel Grand. It also included a public park and access to the beach alongside Lake Michigan. It was, in effect, a black city within a city.

By 1920, this district housed around 93,000 residents (out of 110,000 African-Americans) in some of the worst slums in Chicago with many apartments converted into kitchenettes to accommodate the vastly increased population. At the edges, well-to-do blacks moved away from the slum districts but two factors prevented any significant movement southward or westward. First was a high degree of organized and spontaneous violence aimed specifically at keeping blacks in their place. In 1919, there was a notorious race riot with many brutal confrontations between white and black Chicagoans. This was caused initially by white thugs who entered the Black Belt on bikes and fired weapons haphazardly killing one person and terrorizing the population. The boundaries of the Black Belt were protected by large numbers of black youths who retaliated by attacking white gangs which resulted in thirty-eight deaths (twenty-three black; fifteen white) and over 500 injured.

Fifty-eight black homes were fire-bombed between 1917 and 1921, one every twenty days, as Drake and Cayton documented. Wealthy black entrepreneurs or professionals were particularly targeted so that they would not expand the ghetto. But it was not just violence that forced complete segregation on the Black Belt and turned it into a ghetto. After the early 1920s a 'colour line' (in the words of Du Bois) was established in Chicago which reinforced a highly segregated black community. This racial isolation was reinforced by letter-writing campaigns, church sermons, and neighbourhood housing associations. Restrictive covenants were signed by the residence of each 'white' neighbourhood to ensure that none of their properties would be occupied, leased, or sold to Negroes. These covenants stayed in force in Chicago for two decades.

Well-off residents, repeating the pattern of other ethnic enclaves, would have much preferred to leave the ghetto. Following mass migration, the ghetto became intolerable with even more slum areas created in the wake of deteriorating health, sanitary, and housing conditions. But the ghetto was not merely a slum. It could thrive in other ways which was an unintended consequence of upper- and middle-class black families being forced to stay. During the 'fat years' (1924–9), as Drake and Cayton phrase it, the culture of the ghetto was divided into survival ('staying alive'); popular music, sports, cinema, fashion, consumption ('having a good time'); attending *en masse* one of dozens of churches and smaller church groups ('praising God'); entrepreneurship, professionalization ('getting ahead'); communal and national pride ('advancing the Race').

In other words, the ghetto was both a haven and a hell, as Freeman argues, or a 'promised land' and 'colony' (phrases used in the mass-produced black newspaper, *Chicago Defender*). This doubleness (both positive and negative) relates the black ghetto to the 'involuntary' Italian ghettos (which were both modern and tribal) as scholars writing on Detroit, Buffalo, Philadelphia, and Pittsburgh recognized when they spoke of the 'invisible walls' surrounding the 'dark ghetto'. Drake and Cayton even referred to the 'invisible barbed-wire fence' surrounding Chicago's South Side—a reference to racially segregated Nazi ghettos—when, as they well knew, the ghetto was actually circumscribed by railroad tracks on either side of the long triangle. That is why Drake and Cayton did not labour the Nazi-analogy and, eventually, rejected the word 'ghetto':

> Misery is not spread evenly over the Black Ghetto for [it] has
> followed the same general pattern of city growth.... [That is why]

'Ghetto' is a harsh term, carrying overtones of poverty and suffering, of exclusion and subordination. In the Midwest Metropolis it is used by civic leaders when they want to shock complacency into action.

Rather than Black Belt or Black Metropolis or Black Ghetto (used interchangeably) Drake and Cayton named the Chicago ghetto 'Bronzeville' so that black neighbourhoods were not reduced to 'poverty and suffering'. That they could not find any one name for the ghetto in over 800 pages is significant, as it was a place which changed greatly throughout time and differed from decade to decade. The 'fat years' were soon followed by the 'lean years' of the Great Depression (1929–39) and by the era of federal intervention which changed the character of the South Side completely.

Bronzeville was the name of the main neighbourhood where black Chicagoans lived and also referred to the famous boxer Joe Lewis (the Bronze Bomber) and the Hollywood actress and singer Lena Horn (the Bronze Nightingale). It may also evoke serendipitously the copper (or bronze) factory which instituted the first 'ghetto' (getto) in Venice. But the poetic imagination was always at the whim of cold-hearted economics. Up until the Great Depression, the Stroll (the name given to State Street between 26th and 39th) showcased established black-owned banks and businesses, and many prestigious musical theatres. The Stroll also included famous residents such as the boxer Jack Johnson, or Oscar De Priest (the first African-American congressman elected from a northern state), or Dr Daniel Hale Williams (who pioneered open-heart surgery). This part real, part mythical, district is what Drake and Clayton meant by the 'Spirit of Bronzeville' or the 'axis of life'—cultural vitality in the widest possible sense—with an early form of public display or 'ghetto fabulousness' at its heart.

The Great Depression changed the face of Bronzeville entirely. Black-owned businesses went bankrupt, jobs disappeared, and cabarets and nightclubs closed. The dream of Bronzeville, a black city within a city, soon turned into a nightmare. Richard Wright, in his bestselling novel *Native Son* (1940) set in the Chicago ghetto, asks 'why do they make us live in one corner of the city…tumbling down with rot'? But the immediate hardship, which resulted in near-starvation for the poorest, was not as consequential as the supposed solution. Immigration into the ghetto fell dramatically throughout the 1930s which reinforced the ghetto boundaries and meant that, by 1940, the ghetto's population was virtually all black. In this depressed and racially concentrated area, the federal government began to intervene in run-down urban districts across the country.

The housing market was a focus of Roosevelt's New Deal with the creation of the Home Owners' Loan Corporation (HOLC) to prevent millions of foreclosures. But black neighbourhoods were considered the most unsafe for assigning cheaper mortgages (known as 'red-lining' or 'red-coding') which meant that ghetto residents, in much of the poorest housing, could only refinance at the highest rates. Such racial profiling, as Freeman shows, was soon institutionalized with the Federal Housing Administration (FHA) arguing that a neighbourhood could only retain 'stability' if properties 'continue to be occupied by the same social and racial standards'. In other words, a majority white residence had, by definition, a good credit risk whereas a majority black residence did not.

The urban historian Arnold Hirsch has argued persuasively that federal intervention with a racial bias created a 'second ghetto' in Chicago from the 1940s to the 1960s. In this period the African-American population rose from 278,000 in 1940 to 813,000 in 1960. At the same time, the federal government created more suburbs, depopulated the centre, and built a massive series of freeways to connect up the centre and periphery by car. At the end of the 1950s the city authorities agreed, after much debate, to build high-rise apartments for the African-Americans left in the inner city which, in one instance, included twenty-eight identical sixteen-storey buildings in groups of three. These Robert Taylor Homes, stretching narrowly for two miles, were the largest housing project in the world replacing the historic slum areas on the South and West Sides. They were built either inside or adjacent to the Black Belt (see Figure 8).

As Dominic Pacyga shows, in his 'biography' of Chicago, more project homes were built in 1960 by the Chicago Housing Association than other years. Large families were given priority and the result was extreme population densities. Robert Taylor Homes, built in 1962, were occupied almost completely by black families—with many more than the official census of 7,000 adults and 21,000 children—which from the start were severely overcrowded. Instead of renewing the black neighbourhoods these vast projects merely expanded and entrenched the ghetto in the South and West Sides. Between 1950 and 1970 the number of blacks in Chicago more than doubled and made up a third of the city's population. Housing projects were built near North Side neighbourhoods as well as the West Side. The second ghetto, as Hirsch puts it, was a 'federally built and supported slum'.

The vast increase of African-Americans in the urban centre was replicated in most major northern cities. Newark and Washington, for instance, became predominantly 'black' during this period. Suburbanization completed this ethnic transfer not least as the suburbs were perceived to be 'white' by ethnic and national groups such as Irish-, Italian-, and Jewish-Americans. Black communities initially welcomed the large housing projects as a form of urban renewal which separated but did not segregate their neighbourhoods. In an exultant headline the *Chicago Defender* trumpeted: 'RACE GETS ONE-FOURTH OF BENEFITS FROM APPROVED FEDERAL HOUSING PROJECTS'. Even Du Bois, militantly against any form of segregation, approved the new housing projects given that they were to replace notorious slums. But by the 1970s the projects became a magnet for violence,

8. Chicago's second ghetto.

deprivation, and gang warfare. They became known as 'black reservations' utterly segregated and isolated from the rest of the city.

Such social and economic deprivation resulted in a series of ferocious urban riots, often provoked by police brutality, throughout the 1960s. These riots (often called insurrections, revolts, or rebellions) commonly took place within the ghetto, burning down commercial buildings, sniping at police, and looting white-owned shops. An egregious example is the Los Angeles riots of August 1965 which left thirty-four dead, 4,000 injured, and $35 million in damaged property. Between July and August 1967, black ghettos in sixty American cities exploded in violence. Chicago followed suit in April 1968 after the assassination of Dr Martin Luther King, Jr, a one-time resident and activist in Chicago.

The so-called 'King Riots' took place in Chicago's West Side where King lived and set up offices for the Chicago Freedom Movement (CFM) in 1966. The CFM, significantly, expanded the civil rights campaign from the south to the north of America. That King chose Chicago, given its long history of racial segregation, was not a coincidence. A day after his murder, black youth took to the streets and King's message of non-violence sadly evaporated. In a heavy-handed response, the Illinois National Guard placed 4,200 troops around the ghetto which were supplemented by the regular army. As with most other riots, there was widespread arson, sniping at guards and firefighters, and looting. The powerful Chicago Mayor Daley (1955–76), a Democrat, ordered the police to 'shoot to kill' arsonists and 'shoot to maim' looters. Such extremity further divided the city with his white working-class base applauding him and the black community appalled at his punitive response.

By the 1970s, for the first time, more blacks moved south rather than north. With the main demands of the civil rights movement met (the right to vote, to marry non-blacks, and to use public facilities equally), living in the south was often seen as more favourable than living in depressed northern inner cities. Urban black ghettos also began to shrink for other reasons. In response to the federal government-sponsored Kerner Commission—which focused on racial discrimination, widespread deprivation, and segregation as causes of the riots—there was a concerted effort to improve black educational and employment opportunities. By 1980, a third of Chicago's African-American population had moved away from the 'vertical ghetto' (as it was called).

From 1950 to 1980, Bronzeville declined by more than half to 36,000. The African-American community fragmented along class lines leaving the ghetto even more impoverished. Around 800,000 were left in deprived neighbourhoods and were, in the main, the poorest of the poor—stigmatized to this day as an 'underclass'. They were often located in the housing projects until the projects were demolished in the 1990s and the first decade of the new century. In the mid-1980s these high rises were completely neglected in contrast to equivalent buildings for white residents. There was little or no money provided for maintenance for the black community. After years of neglect the projects were commonly infested with cockroaches and rats with no entry halls or working lifts or any meaningful security. Graffiti covered the walls, and stairways were unlit and smelling of human and animal excrement. Ground floor apartments were boarded up to avoid repeat burglaries, and gangs controlled many entrances and exits. The sociologist Loïc Wacquant has called these slum buildings 'hyperghettos'.

By the 1990s, some black communal groups argued that public housing, such as the Henry Hormer homes, were in such disrepair (with half of the apartments unoccupied) that they were in effect already demolished. Other groups resisted the demolition of their homes on the grounds that this was an effective community living in the most difficult of circumstances. They had found a way of living with, and not against, the gangs that occupied the buildings.

Older residents remembered the slum clearances of an earlier period which led to these overpoliced and underfunded neighbourhoods. If the high rises came down, what would replace them and where would they live? Published census data showed that five million African-Americans lived in high-poverty neighbourhoods, compared with 2.5 million white Americans. They well understood that the grass was hardly ever greener elsewhere.

Over two decades, from the 1990s onwards, there was a struggle to demolish the Cabrini-Green housing project on the near North Side of Chicago. Cabrini-Green was located conveniently in the centre of Chicago, near public transport, which was why the city authorities were anxious to 'gentrify' the area by demolishing the eight, fifteen-storey buildings (with around 3,500 apartments). The voices of the occupants have been documented in film and ethnographies to show that the ghetto 'underclass' was not 'pathological' as has often been stated in official and scholarly accounts. Blaming the victims for the underinvestment by the Chicago Housing Association (a pattern repeated in most major cities) is used to 'explain' the breakdown of conventional family ties, widespread drug use, gang control, and high levels of male imprisonment. But communal organizations argued that they had a rich cultural life in these projects, despite the most difficult of circumstances.

As the sociologist Ray Hutchinson asks astutely, if the neighbourhoods and buildings of the historic black ghetto have disappeared then does the Chicago ghetto still exist? Some have concluded that the word 'ghetto' has outlived its usefulness given that poor blacks are concentrated in dispersed neighbourhoods on the South Side and live next to other poor minority groups, such as Latinos or African refugees. Does that mean that poverty and the ghetto are the same? Alternatively, if 'the ghetto' were to encompass African-Americans of all classes and locations then it is merely reduced to a person's 'blackness'. What is clear is that there is no longer a policy of assimilating the ghetto into the urban cityscape which relies on communal welfare provision. Instead, the local and federal policy in the 21st century is one of near-abandonment of the impoverished occupants of the ghetto by dispersing black neighbourhoods so that they can have even less impact on the running of the city.

Harlem

The New York and Chicago ghettos were thought of as opposites almost as soon as they were formed. This can be seen as early as 1927 when Hubert Harrison, writing in the *New York Amsterdam News* (America's oldest black newspaper), compared their economic activities. Harrison, a socialist and black nationalist, was from the Virgin Islands and, like many migrants from the Caribbean, viewed America much more critically than native-born Harlemites. His article was scathing about Harlem's lack of black businesses: 'For all Harlem's bluff and bluster we have no Negro Bank. Chicago has three. Negro business in Harlem still goes on crutches.... Chicago has many streets full of Negro businesses'. No wonder Harrison introduced an 'outdoor university' into Harlem—complementing his indoor 'Harlem School of Social Science'—lecturing on street corners on radical economics, class politics, and African history.

Compared to the boom years of Chicago in the 1920s, Harlem was stifled economically. White New Yorkers owned nearly all of the housing and commerce in Harlem, which was why the black economy could not flourish. Like every other city, rents for housing in black areas were exorbitantly high to take advantage of the vastly increased demand for accommodation after the Great Migration. There were organized groups fighting these high rents. Landlords and estate agents responded by placing black families in 'white' areas (known as 'blockbusting') so that ethnic white New Yorkers would move and the growing black population could be exploited. As early as 1915, the exodus of Italian, Irish, and Jews from Harlem was proceeding apace leaving housing empty, but not their businesses, which remained up to 80 per cent white-owned until the Great Depression.

Chicago was always more rooted in the material and the practical with Bronzeville, despite the best efforts of Drake and Clayton, never quite achieving the symbolic resonance of Harlem. But it is open to question whether the myth of Harlem—known as a 'city within a city', the 'black mecca', or the 'Negro capital of the world'—made it an exception to other black ghettos. Harlem was subject to the same sweeping historical changes—the Great Migrations, the two world wars, the Great Depression, federal funding of segregated public housing—which shaped all other ghettos. If anything, Harlem faced a higher degree of violent white racism at an earlier stage than other black neighbourhoods. Between 1907 and 1911, there were regular pitched battles between white gangs, backed by the police, who wanted to control Harlem's boundaries and were resisted by black youth.

The racist policy of 'containment' (although the six square miles of Harlem was not enclosed) was reinforced during and after World War I as the population of African-Americans (from the southern states and the Spanish Caribbean) increased from around 90,000 to 150,000 between 1910 and 1920. During the following decade Harlemites more than doubled to 320,000. But this rapid increase in population, making Harlem the largest black ghetto in America, resulted in an equally swift deterioration in the overcrowded population caused by the lack of adequate employment and housing. Nonetheless, church leaders in the southern states regarded Harlem as a 'symbol of liberty and the Promised Land to Negroes everywhere' which encouraged yet more mass migration from the south. After all, by 1940 New York had over 10,000 industries which were 11 per cent of all industry in the United States. What could be more attractive than the promise of industrial labour for the Jim Crow south?

Harlem initially was far from being a slum district; its houses were noticeably grander and more attractive than virtually any other black neighbourhood. Their sheer size—built initially for wealthy white colonial families—and boulevard-type avenues embodied the modernity of the 'New Negro' who was at last free from slavery and segregation. But the attractive brownstones of Harlem were also one reason for its descent into slumdom after World War I. Rents were astronomically high in the 1920s because of the sheer numbers needing affordable homes. Soon these large brownstones (which were built to house a family of six or seven) were transformed crudely into tiny kitchenettes for around three times as many occupants. Salaries hardly compensated for these high rents as black Harlemites were confined, in the main, to unskilled labour: as tram or lift operators, dockworkers, porters, or factory labourers for the men; and as domestic labour or, at best, sales clerks for the women.

Well before the Great Depression, Harlem was in decline and led America, according to the local historian Jonathan Gill, in 'poverty, crime, overcrowding, unemployment, juvenile delinquency, malnutrition, and infant and maternal mortality'. The infant mortality rate was twice as high as the rest of the city and the death rate in general nearly matched this figure. Four times as many Harlemites, compared to New Yorkers as a whole, died of tuberculosis and around half the working population were either ill or unemployed. Before 1930, Harlem was a 'profitable slum', as the social historian Gilbert Ofosky puts it, although it was not particularly exceptional in this regard. What is unusual is that the Harlem Renaissance, which does distinguish Harlem from all other ghettos, flowered at the same time as much of it was becoming a slum (see Figure 9).

New York was the centre for literature and publishing in the United States which helped to transform Harlem into a 'Negro mecca' for artists and musicians of all kinds. From the 1920s to

9. Harlem's Renaissance.

the 1930s, imaginative writers as varied as Rudolph Fisher, Langston Hughes, Zora Neale Hurston, Nella Larson, and Claude McKay were to humanize Harlem in their poetry, stories, and fiction. Along with home-grown singers and musicians, such as Thomas 'Fats' Waller and Billie Holiday, Harlem exemplified the Jazz Age by attracting all of the leading jazz performers from Louis Armstrong and Duke Ellington to Bessie Smith and Charlie Parker. As Hughes observed, 'Harlem was like a magnet for New York intellectuals and artists, pulling them from everywhere'. The jazz nation descended on Harlem and resulted in an extraordinary outpouring—from jazz clubs, to speakeasies, to dance halls—which invigorated literary and popular artistry uniquely.

During the Harlem Renaissance, the public library and YMCA became performance spaces for readings of stories and poetry. As Alain Locke was to write, in his manifesto on 'The New Negro' (1925), the 'race capital' Harlem was akin to other capital cities throughout the world where avant-garde artistic movements were born:

In Harlem, Negro life is seizing upon its first chances for group expression and self-determination. It is—or promises to be at least—a race capital.... Harlem has the same role to play for the 'New Negro' as Dublin has had for the New Ireland or Prague for the New Czechoslovakia.

But Locke also makes clear that the arrival of the 'New Negro' was not clear-cut. This modern figure was a 'collaborator and participant in American civilization' as well as someone who must 'preserve and implement [their] own racial traditions'. This duality echoed Du Bois's 1903 characterization of the 'double consciousness' of African-Americans who, because of a society saturated in racism, have a sense of 'one's self through the eyes of others.... An American, a negro... two warring ideals in one dark body'. The Harlem Renaissance aimed to resolve this 'twoness' through a new appreciation of black culture as well as the many lasting transformations of both people and place. But the severe economic downturn, which closed down most of the best known entertainment venues in Harlem, soon undermined these lofty ideals.

In 1936, a year after a violent ghetto uprising, Locke looks back in sadness at Harlem after it was decimated by the Great Depression: 'It is easier to revel in the hardy survivals of Negro art and culture than to contemplate this dark Harlem of semi-starvation, mass exploitation and seething unrest'. Many commentators on Harlem have described its history as a 'tale of two cities'. Starving Harlem and Renaissance Harlem, in other words, can be found in one 'dark body'. The extremity of this division distinguishes Harlem from other black ghettos not least in whether it should be described as a ghetto or not. Chicago was the original ethnographic location for ghetto studies in the United States, but Harlem was the first black neighbourhood where some of its best known inhabitants resisted it being called a 'ghetto'.

Kenneth Clark's *Dark Ghetto: Dilemmas of Social Power* (1965), published a year after the Harlem Riots, is the best known account of Central Harlem's descent into squalor. At the time he was researching the book, half of all households lived at or below the poverty line. *Dark Ghetto* made an enormous impact as it was, quite literally, a *cri de coeur* opening with 'The Cry of the Ghetto' which was a series of quotations from despairing, near-suicidal, inhabitants: 'The way the Man has us, he has us wanting to kill one another'. Clark relies on data from his earlier ethnographic study of Harlem youth and is grounded in what he calls in this work 'pathology and powerlessness'.

For this reason, *Dark Ghetto* makes a continued analogy with Jewish ghettos under Nazism. From the 'The Invisible Wall' of the second chapter to topics hermetically sealed 'inside the ghetto' such as 'power', 'social dynamics', 'psychology', 'pathology', 'schools', and 'black and white'. Taking his cue from Holocaust survivors Viktor Frankl and Bruno Bettelheim, Clark called himself an 'involved observer' as he had an intimate knowledge of Harlem residents as the co-founder (with Dr Mamie Clark) of the Northside Center for Child Development. But the analogy with Nazi ghettos meant that he characterized those living in Harlem as utterly without agency. He also called the ghetto a form of 'colonization' (a term which the Black Power movement took up) and argued that the brutal conditions of the ghetto made its inhabitants 'pathological'.

Clarke's use of ghetto to structure his book, and the resulting view of Harlem's residents as passive or neurotic, rankled with two of Harlem's most eminent residents. Albert Murray was most explicit when he asked in *The Omni-Americans* (1970) that 'following a writer like Clark': 'What useful purpose is really served by confusing segregated housing in the U.S. with the way Jewish life was separated from the gentile world in the days of the old ghettos?' Murray is writing from a broadly humanist perspective that stresses the ability of those in Harlem to assert their own identities and to move and work in and out of the supposed 'ghetto'. He believed, above all, in an expansive 'Omni-America' where blacks could participate in the so-called 'white world'.

A humanist rejection of the 'dark ghetto' was also articulated by Murray's friend, the bestselling novelist Ralph Ellison, who rejected the notion of Harlem as a 'ghetto maze'. The notion of the 'ghetto' prevented black Harlem becoming part of a wider democracy which is, in effect, a 'denial of Negro humanity'. Ellison argued this in an essay called pointedly 'Harlem is Nowhere' (1948). Unlike the Lower East Side of New York, which by the 1940s was already a site of memory for the hundreds of thousands of Jews who once lived there, Ellison and Murray did not want Harlem reduced to a ghetto. It was an irony, not lost on these great writers, that New York's Jews were able to leave the Lower East Side *en masse* but still referred to this ethnic enclave as a 'ghetto'.

For Ellison, the 'Negro ghetto' meant that Negros (using the words of Baldwin) 'piss in the halls and [have] blood on the stairs' which denies the all-too-human 'complexity of Harlem'. Ghetto, from this perspective, is a sociological abstraction which reduced the possibility of rising above such desolation: 'For if Harlem is the scene of the folk-Negro's death agony, it is also the setting of his transcendence'. Ellison's argument with Baldwin (and also Wright) is part of a larger debate concerning the nature of the novel. In his essay 'The Harlem Ghetto' (1948), responding implicitly to Ellison, Baldwin characterized Harlem as a place which was 'constricted' and lacked any form of transcendence: 'All over Harlem, Negro boys and girls are growing into stunted maturity, trying desperately to find a place to stand'. One was a novelist who wanted to transfigure the 'agony' of living, the other was a novelist mired in such harsh realities.

The Harlem Riot of 1964 was the immediate context for *Dark Ghetto* and generated the book's sense of pessimism and loss. The six days of rioting in mid-July was caused by police violence: the shooting of James Powell, a 15-year-old African-American. Virtually all police officers at the time were white. Three hundred students from Powell's school immediately confronted the police and the riot soon turned violent. It spread from Harlem to Queens, to Bedford Stuyvesant and the Bronx, with 4,000 New Yorkers participating. The police station was a target as was general looting and vandalism which focused mainly but not exclusively on 'white' businesses.

Most other riots followed the pattern in Harlem not least in the name of black nationalism or black consciousness as well as civil rights. It was at this point that ghettos were thought of as colonies and were refigured as a place where black solidarity and radical transformation could be achieved. The ghetto was now a fixed point of black identity, as seen in the Black Arts Movement, which was sealed in the blood of those killed in the riots.

The response to the 1960s riots by the federal authorities changed Harlem and most other ghettos beyond recognition. After the riots the federal government invested once again in public housing in the ghettos as we have seen in the case of Chicago and every other major northern city. Historic African-American districts were completely demolished in dozens of cities where riots took place and, worse still, areas which were destroyed in the riots were often left standing as slums. As the black middle classes began to move out of Central Harlem, the 'outcast' population of the black poor increased and, as in all other 'rust belt' cities, were confined to segregated housing projects or dispersed to other impoverished districts.

In the era of deindustrialization, since the 1980s, black ghettos have been deemed to be incapable of contributing to the global economy just as they were once thought to be incapable of contributing to the American economy. The result has been gentrification by aggressive 'heroic' city mayors such as Rudolph

Giuliani (known as 'Mr Global') who reshaped mid-town Manhattan. As the urban historian David Wilson has shown, city planners at this time were mandated to turn this area into a 'nub of affluence'. This included luxury townhouses (reclaiming Harlem's brownstones for the wealthy) and opulent restaurants and supermarkets to match. This 'nub' was to be extended and protected by the police so that, finally, the ghetto would be gentrified out of existence (or as far away from Manhattan as possible). Young black men on bicycles and 'squeegee merchants' were especially targeted by the police. The Harlem ghetto was once called 'the capital of any ghetto town' but how can it be a capital when, like Chicago, it has been changed beyond recognition?

In 2018, Central Harlem was relatively integrated although there were districts, such as East Harlem, where African-Americans and Hispanics remained isolated, jobless, impoverished, and prey to drug culture. The contrast between gentrified areas of large cities such as Philadelphia and Washington and an ongoing ghetto-like existence continues to this day. This is because, as Wacquant argues, mass incarceration acts as a measure of social control on a scale not seen before. The prison houses around 1.4 million blacks and Latinos, which enables ghetto-clearance and gentrification. In 2013, African-Americans and Latinos comprised about 60 per cent of the prison population although together they were only 30 per cent of the national population. With mass incarceration turning the poorest districts into an extension of the prison—or a 'surrogate ghetto'—the poorest of the poor are treated as nothing more than 'human waste'. In such circumstances the continuation of the ghetto in its latest form remains an urgent matter of social justice.

The ghetto today

In Chicago most of the historic sites of the ghetto have disappeared. Bronzeville hardly exists but it has been turned into a 'historic district' with few physical reminders of its past life as a ghetto. Middle-class blacks have invested in making iconic Bronzeville into a site of sacred memory (one among many such memory sites across north-eastern cities). This historic district has been modelled on Drake and Clayton's *Black Metropolis*, which is no longer an ethnography but is now the blueprint for identity formation. Such memory work is in stark contrast to the high levels of police violence, unemployment, infant mortality rates, incarceration, teenage pregnancy, and violent crime which are still part of poor black neighbourhoods.

The gap between actual and imagined ghettos is particularly stark in the United States as the African-American novelist, Percival Everett, has shown. His satire on ghetto identity can be found in *Erasure: A Novel* (2001) where his persona, Thelonious Ellison, self-consciously combines Ralph Ellison with Thelonious Monk, the great Harlem jazz musician. But the middle-class Thelonious Ellison just wants to write versions of the Greek myths which have nothing to do with the Harlem ghetto. This proves to be impossible, as the only novels that are recognized publically by African-American writers are caricatures of the ghetto such as Juanta Mae Jenkins' runaway bestseller *We's Lives in Da Ghetto*. The rave review of this prototypical work of fiction is characteristic:

> Juanta Mae Jenkins has written a masterpiece of African American literature. One can actually hear the voices of her people as they make their way through the experience which is and can only be Black America.

The black American 'experience' follows, predictably, a conventional ghetto narrative concerning 'baby mamas', drug addicts, 'mentally deficients', gang deaths, prostitution, and the 'black matriarchal symbol of strength'. Unable to resist these all-pervasive images, Thelonious Ellison transforms himself into a 'ghetto' writer and publishes *My Pathology*, a pastiche of Wright's *Native Son* with a nod towards the 'pathology' which characterized Clark's *Dark Ghetto* and the 1965 Moynihan Report on the 1960s riots. Everett's *My Pathology* was a typical ghetto parody in the first decade of the new century.

A series of bestselling books had transformed the deprivations of the ghetto into a 'state of mind' rather than a place—*150 Ways to Tell If You Are Ghetto*; *Sckraight from the Ghetto*; *GhettoNation*—as if ghettos no longer existed. In the first decade of the new century, *Saturday Night Live* reinforced the idea of a fantasy ghetto with regular satirical sketches using the punchline *So Ghetto!* These sketches poked fun at the middle classes for aspiring to be more 'ghetto' or authentic, as if poor black populations were nothing more than a series of white perceptions.

A key context for the circulation of these ghetto caricatures was the ubiquity of 'gangsta rap' from the late 1980s onwards. This immensely popular version of hip hop has been rightly described by the musicologist Robin Kelley as 'ghettocentric'. Gangsta rap is generally regarded as less overtly political and more nihilistic than mainstream hip hop. But, as Shelby argues, it is best to recognize that there are 'no sharp boundaries between politics, play, and pleasure' in gangsta rap. Peopled by already 'known' ghetto types, gangsta rap both reinforces and destabilizes such caricatures in equal measure. Song-stories are told from the perspective of the ghetto-dweller but this viewpoint is multiple and could be, as Kelley shows, a 'criminal, the victim of police repression, the teenage father, the crack slanger, the gang banger, the female dominator'. Confusing the singer with the song has caused a good deal of misunderstanding.

When gangsta rappers proclaim themselves to be 'Niggaz' they are invoking a version of the so-called black 'underclass'. The 'Nigga' shows solidarity with other ghetto-dwellers and reflects the widespread distortions of ghetto life as if their life were singular and homogenous. This figure is also starkly different from middle-class blacks (who have abandoned them) and even the hard-working lower classes who are deluded into accepting conventional values. It is not a coincidence that Niggaz Wit Attitudes (NWA), formed in 1987, popularized gangsta rap— which began in New York and Philadelphia—in the context of South-Central Los Angeles (mainly Watts and Compton). After deindustrialization, this area was utterly impoverished in the early 1980s with half of its young and old population unemployed and the average income dropping to near-starvation levels. Crack cocaine was introduced into this economic and social meltdown, which intensified violence between competing gangs who wanted to control the drugs market. The philosopher and activist Cornel West has spoken of the 'monumental eclipse of hope' in such a context and the 'unprecedented collapse of meaning' in response.

For many undereducated, unemployed, disaffected black youth the 'gang bangin' lifestyle' was the only viable means of earning an income. It was this nihilistic and murderous form of money-making that was reflected in the songs of NWA such as 'Straight Outta Compton', 'Gangsta Gangsta', and 'Real Niggaz'. For the majority of residents, as Kelley observes, gang warfare transformed South-Central Los Angeles into a 'militarized landscape' with police helicopters overhead, electronic surveillance, and 'small tanks armed with battering rams' introduced for the first time. This was also the lived experience ('Outta Compton') of Arabian Prince, Dr Dre, Easy E, and Ice Cube. With 'wit', 'attitude', and aggression ('Fuck Tha Police'), NWA was the first of many collective responses to the utter disregard of life and property in the ghetto. Their braggadocio, misogyny, and rampant consumerism reflect back on those outside of the ghetto a grotesque parody of American 'rags to riches' values, which recasts 'capitalism as gangsterism' in Kelley's deft phrase.

For Shelby the 'impure dissent' of gangsta rap is not just an extension of civil disobedience. After all, over two-thirds of gangsta rap is consumed by non-black peoples. But the defiance of mainstream values in this counter-culture illustrates a fundamental breakdown of social 'reciprocity' that needs to be addressed. Shelby is on the side of what he calls 'ghetto abolitionism' which, he believes, is a problem not of black poverty but of basic justice. This is because the ghetto is a 'sign that American social order is profoundly unjust'. From this perspective, structural changes are needed in welfare, housing, employment opportunities, school investment, and health services to name the most obvious causes of ghetto deprivation. After a century of racialized segregation, the call for ghetto abolition in America may no longer be a revolutionary act but an urgent necessity.

Chapter 6
The global ghetto

At the end of his essay on 'The Grey Zone', Primo Levi looked back at the figure of Chaim Rumkowski, the leader of the Łódź ghetto who collaborated with the Nazis. He concluded the essay by arguing that Rumkowski was 'so dazzled by power and prestige' that he forgot 'our essential fragility'. After this summary, Levi relates this 'fragility' to the world as a whole:

> Willingly or not we come to terms with power, forgetting that
> we are all in the ghetto, that the ghetto is walled in, that outside
> the ghetto reign the lords of death and that close by the train
> is waiting.

Throughout history, ghetto-dwellers have perceived their enforced home as a world unto itself. Oskar Rosenfeld, in the Łódź ghetto, thought that the ghetto was a 'natural phenomenon like the creation of the world': 'In the beginning, God created the ghetto'. During the early modern period ghettos were commonly thought of as 'Jewish cities' or as 'Little Jerusalems'. By the start of the 20th century, the Lower East Side of New York was described as the 'metropolis of the ghettos of the world'. During the Nazi period, Jews, left destitute by draconian racial laws, lived within the 'invisible walls' of the ghetto. After World War I, African-Americans realized that they were destined to be confined for decades to urban ghettos which they thought of as 'black cities' or 'cities within a city', with Harlem as the 'black mecca' or the 'Negro capital of the world'.

There is, needless to say, a fundamental difference between inhabitants of the ghetto thinking of their enforced confines as a world unto itself and Levi's sense of a ghetto-like world ('we are all in the ghetto'). But what is significant is how quickly the idea of the ghetto can be universalized and encompass so much more than its local circumstances. Today, this is particularly evident when the ghetto is treated merely as a free-floating metaphor. Books are written with titles such as *The World is a Ghetto: Race and Democracy since World War Two* (2001) by Howard Winant without even mentioning the word ghetto (or equivalent urban enclaves) in the work. Such studies remind us that ghetto is a word which, if we are not careful, can be everywhere (on the title page) and nowhere (in the book).

As Bruce Haynes and Ray Hutchinson have contended, the 21st century is a time when American hip-hop culture (especially gangsta rap) has influenced the inhabitants (from Moscow to Soweto) of *banlieues, barrios, degradati, favela, villa miseria,* slums, townships, camps, and reservations (see Figure 10). From 'ghetto' storefronts, to hip-hop radio stations, to rap performances, disenfranchised youth of all creeds and colours have appropriated a ghettocentric 'gangsta' rap culture to depict their specific urban, segregated landscape. But these ubiquitous ghettos (influenced by South-Central Los Angeles) are no more than metaphors for particular local conditions.

An example of this uneasy appropriation is the township of Soweto near Johannesburg in South Africa. During the era of apartheid (1948–94) the long-playing record was the most important means of transcultural communication. Black South Africans were particularly influenced by African-American 'gangster' culture beginning with film and culminating with hip-hop. But this is not a case of straightforward appropriation or

10. Soweto.

of soft colonialism, as others have argued. Sowetan rap musicians have created the 'sound of the ghetto' in their own image, which combines indigenous musical forms with their own experiences. It is, like its American counterpart, overwhelmingly masculine, often misogynist, in a misguided response to the lack of male power in the public sphere for black and Asian men. This form of home-grown rap is called *kwaito* and was the first black-controlled popular music form after apartheid. According to Angela Impey:

> Coloured youth were drawn to Black American rap and hip hop artists such as Ice-T, Public Enemy, and Niggaz wit Attitudes. The music prompted the formation of local coloured groups who appropriated images of American hard-core rap.

But these responses to rap and hip-hop were, as the ethno-musicologist Zine Magubane shows, pioneered by a variety of stratified racial groups in many different places (here so-called 'Cape coloureds'). Many *kwaito* songs are sung in the vernacular—Zulu, Xhosa, Tswana, or Sotho—with no need to create an alternative 'black' English vernacular, as in American rap. These songs combine a 'local flavour' (so as to connect with their communities) as well as a ghettocentric feeling of displacement. Around 75 per cent of the black population in South Africa are under 25 which makes it a large market for *kwaito*/hip-hop. The marketing board for Soweto at one time rebranded the township as a 'ghetto' for both foreign tourists and locals. But most black South African youth value indigenous cultural forms even while basing their fashion style (baseball caps, baggy pants, gold jewellery) and general sense of dislocation on black Americans. This combination of local and global speaks to the complexity of the word ghetto as it travels far and wide.

Two general approaches to ghettoization illustrate this point. Carl Nightingale has published a global history of segregation in urban contexts across seventy centuries. This monumental account includes various histories of the ghetto but just as one aspect of segregation in general (see Figure 11). In that way, the social historian Nightingale can look at particular ghetto formations, as we have done in this book, rather than assume that all forms of segregation are the same as ghettoization. Zygmunt Bauman, on the other hand, argues that the ghetto rather than segregation is the norm in our 'liquid modern' world: 'The ghetto serves not as a reservoir of disposable industrial labour but a mere dumping ground for those for whom the surrounding society has no economic or political use'. But not all impoverished districts, segregated by wealth, are called ghettos by their residents. *Banlieues*, *barrios*, *degradati*, *favela*, and *villa miseria* all prefer French and Spanish equivalents rather than German or English. Universal definitions such as Bauman's, in other words, need to be qualified.

The ghetto, as we have seen throughout the book, is a travelling concept. Up until the present day, however, its forms of travel have been limited to occupants of the ghetto. Those in early modern ghettos looked back to the relative freedom of the Jewish quarters;

11. Urban segregation.

the imaginary ghettos of the 19th century refashioned past ghettos so that they were located in Eastern as opposed to Western Europe. By the 20th century, ethnic enclaves were described as ghettos, going back to historic ghettos. The return to 'medieval' origins was a myth taken up by the Nazis and also by many victims of ghettoization in their diaries and memoirs. By the second half of the 20th century, in African-American neighbourhoods, the idea of the ghetto was multidirectional going back to the Italian peninsula and ethnic enclaves and across to Nazi ghettos. African-Americans had a choice of analogies most suited (or not) to their current experience of ghettoization. Like Jews in the 19th century, those black middle classes who had recently left the ghetto chose to imagine past ghettos as sacred sites of memory.

Today's global ghetto complicates matters further. As we have seen in the case of Soweto, the ghetto now combines local experience with a global style. If 'the ghetto' is to have any conceptual significance then it needs to be returned to the realm of ethnography or to the perspective of those whose lives have been shaped by class and racial segregation. To this extent, it is crucial to listen to those 'outcasts' who resist their plight by appropriating and utilizing the history and culture of the ghetto.

The appropriation of the Warsaw ghetto is a good example of how the limited travels of the ghetto in earlier centuries have expanded to other (hitherto unghettoized) regions of the world today. The Warsaw ghetto, as a site for mass murder and resistance, was an early symbol of the Holocaust before the Jewish genocide was named as such. This can be seen in a visit to Warsaw by W. E. B. Du Bois who had been a student at the University of Berlin. Du Bois had reported on Nazi Germany in 1936 but did not understand the nature of the Jewish genocide before his trip to Warsaw. This was his third visit to Poland, although he had travelled extensively around Nazi Germany and had witnessed antisemitism first-hand. But Du Bois was transformed completely after seeing the remains of the Warsaw ghetto in 1952:

> My view of the Warsaw ghetto was not so much a clearer understanding of the Jewish problem in the world as it was a real and more complete understanding of the Negro problem....So that the ghetto of Warsaw helped me to emerge from a certain social provincialism into a broader conception of what the fight against race segregation, religious discrimination and the oppression by wealth had to become if civilization was going to triumph and broaden the world.

What was particularly 'hard' for Du Bois to learn is that the 'problem of slavery, emancipation and caste' was not just a matter of the 'colour line' as he had long since argued. Instead, the 'race problem in which I was interested cut across lines of colour...and reached all sorts of people and caused endless evil to all men'. This extension of the 'colour line', as the cultural theorist Michael Rothberg has argued, shows how mutidirectional histories—from African-American ghettos to Warsaw and back again—expands an understanding of racial oppression so that each ghetto becomes part of a broader history. Rothberg contrasts the multidirectional expansion of knowledge, the theme of this book, with a zero-sum approach to ghettoization, where one history of the ghetto replaces another. Black nationalists, who disagreed with Du Bois's cosmopolitanism, for instance, refused to draw on Jewish analogies with regard to the African-American ghetto but preferred to think of ghettoization as a form of colonialism or apartheid so as to associate their struggle not with 'whitened' Jews but with the colonized peoples of the world.

The difference between Du Bois and black nationalists indicates that a zero-sum approach to the history of ghettoization is most likely when two histories are in conflict with each other. This is particularly true with regard to Israel-Palestine where, in the past decade, the Gaza Strip has been repeatedly compared to the

Warsaw ghetto. Bauman, whose wife Janina Bauman escaped the Warsaw ghetto, has, for instance, argued that: 'the idea of a separation wall as a solution [to the conflict with the Palestinians] would not have occurred to Israeli leaders were it not for ghetto walls being so deeply ingrained in the Jewish collective memory'. Many Palestinian nationalists have compared themselves to 'new Jews' living in a ghetto (Gaza) but this merely replaces one history of the ghetto with another. To attain something like Du Bois's multidirectional enlargement of the history of ghettoization Jews and Palestinians need, ultimately, to recognize each other's history of suffering which includes different kinds of enforced detention and impoverishment.

The imposition of the term 'ghetto' on a powerless population is crucially different from the self-appropriation of 'ghetto' as a form of cultural expression. For Eastern European Jews, during the 19th century, the ghetto was an alien term (from the German language) which was imposed on the Pale of the Settlement in Imperial Russia housing millions of Jews. Jewish townships in this reservation (as we would call it today) were known by their dwellers as *shtetls* and were not known as ghettos. This term only made sense with reference back to the age of the ghetto. But that was a Western European history which had little in common with the history of East European Jews.

The imposition of the term 'ghetto' on a stigmatized population is, ultimately, an expression of power and superiority. An example of such an imposition can be found in present-day Denmark which has, in response to its Muslim citizens, enshrined in official documents the use of 'ghetto' in relation to its schools and minority ethnic neighbourhoods. Denmark may be following Germany in this regard. In the 1990s, the term ghetto once again came to prominence in relation to the assimilation (or not) of Muslim Turks. As the cultural historian Maria Stehle has shown, Germany has returned to earlier uses of the ghetto (which once saturated the German language) in 'debates over the ghettoization of neighbourhoods, ghetto schools, honour killings, and the wearing of headscarves'. German-Turks have been belittled as ghetto-beings in the way that German-Jews were once defamed. At the same time many German-Turks have appropriated the term ghetto ('getto') and worn it as a badge of honour. Not unlike post-apartheid South Africans, they have co-opted rap and hip-hop from the United States (in music, film, and fiction) but with their own German-Muslim twist.

The element of power, in accounting for those who use the word ghetto, has not changed across time. Phrases such as 'gourmet ghettos' or 'gated ghettos' or 'ghetto golf' empty the word of any meaning as they are promoted by those with social power. The reason for making distinctions between the powerful and the powerless is so that we can understand the way that 'ghetto' can both embolden and coerce those without power. Ethically we need to be on the side of those who are emboldened by the word ghetto for it to remain useful and relevant. With such distinctions we can decide whether ghetto is a term of abuse or enables social justice; whether it transcends mere class division; and whether its history across centuries is a resource for those living in present-day ghettos. But it is ultimately up to each reader, in sympathy with ghetto-dwellers past and present, to decide on the usefulness and relevance of the concept and its many-layered histories.

References

This section includes works cited or drawn on in the text in alphabetical order. Page numbers refer to direct quotations, specific information, as well as pages consulted.

Chapter 1: Why ghetto?

Fritz Backhaus et al. (eds), *The Frankfurt 'Judengasse': Jewish Life in an Early Modern German City* (London: Vallentine Mitchell, 2010), pp. 1–2, 5–6, 41–6.

Mitchell Duneier, *Ghetto: The Invention of a Place, the History of an Idea* (New York: Farrar, Straus and Giroux, 2015), pp. ix–xii, 5–7, 11–25, 220–2.

Wendy Z. Goldman and Joe William Trotter, Jr (eds), *The Ghetto in Global History: 1500 to the Present* (London: Routledge, 2018), pp. 1–19, 24–9, 31–7, 40–2, 47, 57–68, 74–88.

Ray Hutchinson and Bruce D. Haynes (eds), *The Ghetto: Contemporary Global Issues and Controversies* (Boulder, CO: Westview Press, 2012), pp. vii–viii, xxxvii, 1–31.

Daniel B. Schwartz, *Ghetto: The History of a Word* (Cambridge, MA: Harvard University Press, 2019), pp. 1–8, 12–16, 49–51.

Chapter 2: The Age of the Ghetto

Benjamin Arbel, *Trading Nations: Jews and Venetians in the Early Modern Eastern Mediterranean* (Leiden: E. J. Brill, 1995), pp. 1–12, 13–28, 55–76, 169–94.

Salo W. Baron, 'Ghetto and Emancipation', *Menorah* 14 (1928): 515–26, in Leo W. Schwarz (ed.), *The Menorah Treasury: Harvest of Half a Century* (Philadelphia: Jewish Publication Society of America, 1964), pp. 50–63.

Robert Bonfil, *Jewish Life in Renaissance Italy* (Los Angeles, CA: University of California Press, 1994), pp. 24, 68–77.

Charles Burroughs, 'Opacity and Transparence: Networks and Enclaves of the Rome of Sixtus V', *RES* 41 (Spring 2002): 56–71.

Robert C. David and Benjamin Ravid, *The Jews of Early Modern Venice* (Baltimore: The Johns Hopkins University Press, 2001), pp. 9–16.

Eric R. Durstler, *Venetians in Constantinople: Nation, Identity, and Coexistence in the Early Modern Mediterranean* (Baltimore: The Johns Hopkins University Press, 2006), pp. 103–12.

Ferdinand Gregorovius, *The Ghetto and the Jews of Rome* (New York: Schocken Books, 1966), pp. 86–90.

Jonathan I. Israel, *European Jewry in the Age of Mercantilism 1550–1750* (Oxford: Oxford University Press, 1989), pp. 12–18, 59–61, 94.

David Philipson, *Old European Jewries* (Philadelphia: Jewish Publication Society of America, 1894), pp. 125–6, 146.

Brian Pullman, *The Jews of Europe and the Inquisition of Venice 1550–1670* (Oxford: Basil Blackwell, 1983), pp. xiii–xiv, 4, 150, 166–7.

Sara Reguer, *The Jews of Italy* (Boston: Academic Studies Press, 2013), pp. 81–110.

E. Natalie Rotham, *Brokering Empire: Trans-Imperial Subjects between Venice and Istanbul* (Ithaca, NY: Cornell University Press, 2012), pp. 49–53.

David Ruderman (ed.), *Essential Papers on Jewish Culture in Renaissance and Baroque Italy* (New York: New York University Press, 1992), pp. 1–39.

David Ruderman, 'The Cultural Significance of the Ghetto in Jewish History', in David Meyers and William Rowe (eds), *From Ghetto to Emancipation* (Scranton: University of Scranton Press, 1997), pp. 1–16.

Richard Sennett, *Flesh and Stone: The Body and the City in Western Civilization* (New York: W. W. Norton and Company, 1994), p. 228.

Stefanie B. Siegmund, *The Medici State and the Ghetto of Florence: The Construction of an Early Modern Jewish Community* (Stanford, CA: University of Stanford Press, 2006), pp. 9, 18–25, 30–1, 61–6, 132–3, 203, 223, 231, 407–12.

Kenneth Stow, *Theater of Acculturation: The Roman Ghetto in the 16th Century* (Seattle: University of Washington Press, 2001), pp. 2–38, 42–5, 62–6.

Kenneth Stow (trans.), *Cum Nimis Absurdum* (1555), in *Catholic Thought and Papal Jewry Policy* (Philadelphia: Jewish Publication Society of America, 1977), pp. 3–21.

Hermann Vogelstein, *Rome: Jewish Communities Series* (Philadelphia: Jewish Publication Society of America, 1940), pp. 263–73, 276–86.

Chapter 3: Ghettos of the imagination

Steven E. Aschheim, *Brothers and Strangers: The East European Jew and German Jewish Consciousness, 1800–1923* (Madison, WI: The University of Wisconsin Press, 1982), pp. 24–31.

Berthold Auerbach, *Das Ghetto* (1837), in Daniel B. Schwartz (trans.), *Ghetto: The History of a Word* (Cambridge, MA: Harvard University Press, 2019), pp. 67–79.

Abraham Cahan, *Yekl & The Imported Bridegroom and Other Stories of the New York Ghetto* (New York: Dover, 1896), pp. vi, 12–21, 38, 44, 89.

Abraham Cahan, *The Education of Abraham Cahan* (Philadelphia: Jewish Publication Society of America, 1969), p. 355.

Jules Chametsky, *From the Ghetto: The Fiction of Abraham Cahan* (Amherst, MA: The University of Massachusetts Press, 1977), pp. 25, 48–51, 53–5, 57–74.

Richard I. Cohen, *Jewish Icons: Art and Society in Modern Europe* (Los Angeles, CA: University of California Press, 1998), pp. 154–85.

Karl Emil Franzos, *The Jews of Barnow: Stories* (London: M.W. MacDowall, 1877), pp. 2–8, 34, 106–7, 127–8, 133.

Hutchins Hapgood, *The Spirit of the Ghetto* (New York: Funk and Wagnalls, 1902), p. 5.

Heinrich Heine, *The Rabbi of Bacherach* (1840) and 'Prologue' to Leopold Kompert, *Scenes from the Ghetto* (1848), in Anne Fuchs and Florian Krobb (trans. and eds), *Ghetto Writing: Traditional and Eastern Jewry in German-Jewish Literature from Heine to Hilsenrath* (Rochester, NY: Camden House, 1999), pp. 4–6, 46–53, 85–8.

Arthur Hertzberg (ed.), *The Zionist Idea* (New York: Atheneum, 1976), p. 238.

Jonathan M. Hess, *Middlebrow Literature and the Making of German-Jewish Identity* (Stanford, CA: Stanford University Press, 2010), pp. 72–110.

Leopold Kompert, *Scenes from the Ghetto: Studies in Jewish Life* (London: Remington and Co., 1882), pp. 3–45.

Leopold Kompert, 'The Pedlar' (1849), in Jonathan M. Hess, Maurice Samuels, and Nadia Valman (trans. and eds), *Nineteenth-Century Jewish Literature* (Stanford, CA: Stanford University Press, 2013), pp. 25–63.

Wayne Miller, *A Gathering of Ghetto Writers: Irish, Italian, Jewish, Black, and Puerto Rican* (New York: New York University Press, 1972), pp. 4–9.

Edna Nashon (ed.), *From the Ghetto to the Melting Pot: Israel Zangwill's Jewish Plays* (Detroit: Wayne State University Press, 2006), pp. 5–28, 72–84.

David Philipson, *Old European Jewries* (Philadelphia: Jewish Publication Society of America, 1894), pp. 220–51.

Jacob A. Riis, *How the Other Half Lives: Studies among the Tenements* (New York: Charles Scribner's Sons, 1889), pp. 89, 91.

Moses Rischin (ed.), *Grandma Never Lived in America: The New Journalism of Abraham Cahan* (Bloomington, IN: Indiana University Press, 1985), pp. xvii–xliv, 513–16.

Peter I. Rose (ed.), *The Ghetto and Beyond: Essays on Jewish Life in America* (New York: Random House, 1969), pp. 3–4.

Miriam Roshwald, *Ghetto, Shtetl, or Polis: The Jewish Community in the Writings of Karl Emil Franzos, Sholom Aleichem, and Shmuel Yosef Agnon* (Maryland: Wildside Press, 1997), pp. 5–18, 27–30, 54, 150–1.

Esther Schor, *Emma Lazarus* (New York: Schocken Books, 2006), pp. 166–72.

W. G. Sebald, 'Westwärts—Ostwärts', *Literatur und Kritik* 24 (1989): 161–77.

Maurice Simon (ed.), *Speeches, Articles and Letters of Israel Zangwill* (London: The Sonico Press, 1937), p. 27.

Daniel Stauben, *Letters on Alsatian Manners* (1849), in Maurice Samuels (trans.), *Inventing the Israelite: Jewish Fiction in Nineteenth-Century France* (Stanford, CA: Stanford University Press, 2010), pp. 1–36, 193–238.

Andrew Whitehead and Jerry White, *London Fictions* (Nottingham: Five Leaves Publications, 2013), pp. 31–41.

Hana Wirth-Nesher (ed.), *The Cambridge History of Jewish American Literature* (Cambridge: Cambridge University Press, 2016), pp. 50, 87–103.

Israel Zangwill, *Children of the Ghetto: A Study of a Peculiar People* (1892) ed. and intro. Meri-Jane Rochelson (Detroit: Wayne State University Press, 1998), pp. 13, 15, 20, 283, 433, 491, 502.

Chapter 4: Nazism and the ghetto

Alan Adelson and Robert Lapides (eds), *Łódź Ghetto: Inside a Community under Seige* (New York: Viking Penguin, 1989), pp. xi–xix, 15, 35–7, 45, 51–5, 87, 107, 143, 206–8, 231–5, 328–31.

Zygmunt Bauman, *Modernity and the Holocaust* (Cambridge: Polity, 1989), pp. 117–28.

Christopher Browning, *The Origins of the Final Solution: The Evolution of Nazi Jewish Policy 1939–1942* (London: Arrow Books, 2005), pp. 112–28, 153–6, 261, 330–3, 416–21.

David Cesarani, *The Final Solution* (London: Macmillan, 2016), pp. 270–3, 331–48, 354–6, 502–8, 606–17.

Tim Cole, *Holocaust City: The Making of a Jewish Ghetto* (London: Routledge, 2003), pp. 25–48.

Israel Gutman, *Resistance: The Warsaw Ghetto Uprising* (Boston: Houghton Mifflin, 1994), pp. 146, 150–3, 163, 207, 215, 255–9.

Gordon J. Horwitz, *Ghettostadt: Łódź and the Making of a Nazi City* (Cambridge, MA: Harvard University Press, 2008), pp. 124–40, 157–8, 162–75.

Samuel D. Kassow (ed.), *In Those Nightmarish Days: The Ghetto Reportage of Peretz Opoczynski and Josef Zelkowicz* (New Haven: Yale University Press, 2005), pp. 146, 150–3, 163, 207, 215, 255–9.

Primo Levi, 'The Grey Zone' (1986), in Raymond Rosenthal (trans.), *The Drowned and the Saved* (London: Michael Joseph, 1988), pp. 46–8.

Mark Mazower, *Hitler's Empire: Nazi Rule in Occupied Europe* (London: Penguin Books, 2008), p. 393.

Dan Michman (trans.), Joachim Prinz, 'Lecture (1935)', Reinhard Heydrich, *Schnellbrief* (1939), and Friedrich Übelhör, 'Memo on the Łódź Ghetto (1939)', in *The Emergence of Jewish Ghettos During the Holocaust* (Cambridge: Cambridge University Press, 2011), pp. 31–5, 38–9, 43–4, 66–75, 89, 136, 155.

Daniel B. Schwartz, *Ghetto: The History of a Word* (Cambridge, MA: Harvard University Press, 2019), pp. 130–8.

Hermann Vogelstein, *Rome: Jewish Communities Series*
(Philadelphia: Jewish Publication Society of America, 1940),
pp. xi–xiii.

Zoë Waxman, *Writing the Holocaust: Identity. Testimony,
Representation* (Oxford: Oxford University Press, 2006), pp. 11–19.

Chapter 5: The ghetto in America

James Baldwin, *Collected Essays* (New York: Library of America,
1998), pp. 53, 293, 742.

Bertice Berry and Joan Coker, *Sckraight from the Ghetto* (New York:
St Martin's Griffin, 1996).

Herb Boyd (ed.), *The Harlem Reader* (New York: Three Rivers Press,
2003), p. 50.

Michelle R. Boyd, *Jim Crow Nostalgia: Reconstructing Race in
Bronzeville* (Minneapolis: University of Minnesota Press, 2008),
pp. xxi–xxv, 82–97, 99–100, 102–3, 155–63.

Todd Boyd, *The New H.N.I.C. The Death of Civil Rights and the
Reign of Hip Hop* (New York: New York University Press, 2004),
pp. 50–6.

John F. Callahan (ed.), *The Collected Essays of Ralph Ellison* (New
York: The Modern Library, 2003), pp. 322, 326, 730.

Kenneth B. Clark, *Dark Ghetto: Dilemmas of Social Power* (New York:
Harper and Row, 1965), pp. xvii–xxii, 2, 11, 15, 45, 56, 79, 186,
222–3, 238–9.

Cora Daniels, *GhettoNation: A Journey into the Land of Bling and the
Home of the Shameless* (New York: Doubleday, 2007).

St Clair Drake and Horace R. Cayton, *Black Metropolis: A Study of
Negro Life in a Northern City* (Chicago: Chicago University Press,
1945), pp. 61, 78–89, 90, 174–80, 383–97, 433–7, 529, 589, 597,
714–20, 733–8, 760, 766.

Percival Everett, *Erasure* (London: Faber, 2001), pp. 3–4, 46.

Lance Freeman, *A Haven and a Hell: The Ghetto in Black America*
(New York: Columbia University Press, 2019), pp. 1–10, 58, 71–80,
91–2, 100, 134–7, 235–6, 243–8, 253–4.

Jonathan Gill, *Harlem: The Four Hundred Year History from Dutch
Village to Capital of Black America* (New York: Grove Press, 2011),
pp. 227, 298, 320, 329–33, 334–60, 385–464.

Nat Hentoff (ed.), *Black Anti-Semitism and Jewish Racism* (New
York: Schocken Books, 1969), pp. xiv–xvii.

Arnold R. Hirsch, *Making the Second Ghetto: Race & Housing in Chicago 1940–1960* (Chicago: University Chicago Press, 1998), pp. vii–xix, 1–10, 226 259–75.

Ray Hutchinson and Bruce D. Haynes (eds), *The Ghetto: Contemporary Global Issues and Controversies* (Boulder, CO: Westview Press, 2012), pp. xxvi–xxxvi, 123–4, 125–34, 305–11, 318–24.

Robin D. G. Kelley, *Race Rebels: Culture, Politics, and the Black Working-Class* (New York: The Free Press, 1994), pp. 185–94, 196–7, 200–14.

Nicholas Lemann, *The Promised Land: The Great Migration and How it Changed America* (New York: Vintage Books, 1991), pp. 343–53.

Richard J. Meister, *The Black Ghetto: Promised Land or Colony* (Lexington, MA: D. C. Heath and Company, 1972).

Albert Murray, *Collected Essays and Memoirs* (New York: Library of America 1970), pp. 67–8.

Gilbert Ofosky, *Harlem: The Making of a Ghetto* (New York, Harper Torchbooks, 1963), pp. 17, 40–3, 84, 87–123, 127–31, 132–3, 136, 137–49, 178, 187, 189–201.

Dominic A. Pacyga, *Chicago: A Biography* (Chicago: University of Chicago Press, 2009), pp. 204–7, 264, 270, 290–3, 315, 328–58, 361, 392.

Tommie Shelby, *Dark Ghettos: Injustice, Dissent, and Reform* (Cambridge, MA: Harvard University Press, 2016), pp. 1, 259, 275–8.

Eric J. Sundquist, *Strangers in the Land: Blacks, Jews, Post-Holocaust America* (Cambridge, MA: Harvard University Press, 2005), pp. 391–2.

Monique M. Taylor, *Harlem between Heaven and Hell* (Minneapolis: University of Minnesota Press, 2002), pp. 5–7, 8–12, 16, 17–23, 86, 129–35, 168.

Sudhir Venkatesh, *American Project: The Rise and Fall of a Modern Ghetto* (Cambridge, MA: Harvard University Press, 2000), pp. 1–12.

Loïc Wacquant, *Urban Outcasts: A Comparative Sociology of Advanced Marginality* (Cambridge: Polity, 2008), pp. 1–12, 53, 75–108.

Shawn Wayans, *150 Ways to Tell if You Are Ghetto* (New York: Dell Publishing, 1997).

Cornel West, *Race Matters* (Boston: Beacon Press, 1993), p. 12.

William Julius Wilson, *The Truly Disadvantaged: The Inner City, the Underclass, and Public Policy* (Chicago: Chicago University Press, 1987).

David Wilson, *Cities and Race: America's New Black Ghetto* (New York: Routledge, 2007), pp. 3–4, 7, 9, 13, 15–18, 19–20, 24, 26–7, 37–8, 44–6, 73, 142.

Louis Wirth, *The Ghetto* (Chicago: Chicago University Press, 1928), pp. 6, 117–19, 128–30, 241–4, 263–8, 282–6, 290–1.

Richard Wright, *Native Son* (London: Vintage Books, 2000), p. 164.

Chapter 6: The global ghetto

Dipannita Basu and Sidney J. Lemelle, *The Vinyl Ain't Final: Hip Hop and the Globalization of Black Popular Culture* (London: Pluto Press, 2006), pp. 208–29.

Zygmunt Bauman, *Community* (Cambridge: Polity, 2001), p. 120.

Ray Hutchinson and Bruce D. Haynes (eds), *The Ghetto: Contemporary Global Issues and Controversies* (Boulder, CO: Westview Press, 2012), pp. 159–90.

Angela Impey, 'Resurrecting the Flesh? Reflections on Women in Kwaito', *Agenda* 49 (2001): 45.

Primo Levi, 'The Grey Zone' (1986), in Raymond Rosenthal (trans.), *The Drowned and the Saved* (London: Michael Joseph, 1988), pp. 50–1.

Carl H. Nightingale, *Segregation: A Global History of Divided Cities* (Chicago: Chicago University Press, 2012).

Michael Rothberg, *The Implicated Subject: Beyond Victims and Perpetrators* (Stanford: Stanford University Press, 2019), pp. 126–31.

Avner Shapira: 'Interview with Zygmunt Bauman on the Eve of his Visit to Israel', *Haaretz Newspaper*, 16 February 2013.

Maria Stehle, *Ghetto Voices in Contemporary German Culture* (New York: Camden House, 2012), pp. 1–7, 11–17.

Eric J. Sundquist (ed.), *The Oxford W.E.B. Du Bois Reader* (Oxford: Oxford University Press, 1996), p. 472.

Further reading

Chapter 1: Why ghetto?

Many aspects of the ghetto are the subject of libraries of scholarly books. But it is only in recent years that the ghetto has been studied as a whole. See Ray Hutchinson and Bruce D. Haynes (eds), *The Ghetto: Contemporary Global Issues and Controversies* (Boulder, CO: Westview Press, 2012); Mitchell Duneier, *Ghetto: The Invention of a Place, the History of an Idea* (New York: Farrar, Straus and Giroux, 2015); Wendy Z. Goldman and Joe William Trotter, Jr (eds), *The Ghetto in Global History: 1500 to the Present* (London: Routledge, 2018); Daniel B. Schwartz, *Ghetto: The History of a Word* (Cambridge, MA: Harvard University Press, 2019).

Chapter 2: The Age of the Ghetto

Along with the references to this chapter, see Cecil Roth, *The History of the Jews of Italy* (Philadelphia: Jewish Publication Society of America, 1946); Roberta Curiel and Bernard Dov Cooperman, *The Ghetto of Venice* (London: Tauris Parke Books, 1990); Kenneth Stow, *Jewish Life in Early Modern Rome: Challenge, Conversion, and Private Life* (London: Ashgate, 2007); Francesca Trivellato, *The Familiarity of Strangers: The Sephardic Diaspora, Livorno, and Cross-Cutural Trade in the Early Modern Period* (New Haven: Yale University Press, 2009); Benjamin Ravid, *Studies on the Jews of Venice, 1382–1797* (London: Ashgate, 2003); Mary Laven, *Virgins of Venice* (London: Viking, 2002).

Chapter 3: Ghettos of the imagination

Along with the references to this chapter, see Leopold Kompert, *Christian and Leah and Other Ghetto Stories* (London: J.M. Dent and Co., 1895); Leopold von Sacher-Masoch, *A Light for Others and Other Jewish Tales from Galicia* (Riverside, CA: Ariadne Press, 1994); Israel Cohen, *Literature in the Ghetto* (London: W. Speaight & Sons, 1903); Meri-Jane Rochelson's *A Jew in the Public Arena: The Career of Israel Zangwill* (Detroit: Wayne State University Press, 2009); David Glover, *Literature, Immigration and Diaspora in Fin-de-Siècle England* (Cambridge: Cambridge University Press, 2012); Moses Hess, *Rome and Jerusalem: The Last National Question* [1862] (New York: Bloch Publishing Company, 1918); Abraham Cahan, *The Rise of David Levinsky* (New York: Harper, 1917); Hana Wirth-Nesher, *Call it English: The Languages of Jewish American Literature* (Princeton: Princeton University Press, 2008).

Chapter 4: Nazism and the ghetto

Along with the references to the chapter, see Philip Friedman, 'The Jewish Ghettos of the Nazi Era', *Jewish Social Studies* 16 (1954): 61–87 for a brief introduction to the topic. A comprehensive description of over 1,000 Nazi ghettos can be found in two contrasting encyclopedias: *The Yad Vashem Encyclopedia of the Ghettos during the Holocaust* (Jerusalem: Yad Vashem, 2009) (in two volumes) and *The United States Holocaust Memorial Museum Encyclopedia of Camps and Ghettos 1933–1945* (Bloomington, IL: Indiana University Press, 2012) (in two volumes).

Chapter 5: The ghetto in America

The ghetto in America has been a scholarly topic for nearly as long as ghettos have existed in the United States. Along with the references to the chapter, see Joe T. Darden (ed.), *The Ghetto: Readings with Interpretations* (New York: Kennikat Press, 1981) for a bibliography of the flood of ethnographic research up until the 1970s. For a present-day perspective on the continuing history of the American ghetto, see Douglas S. Massey and Nancy A. Denton, *American Apartheid: Segregation and the Making of the Underclass* (Cambridge, MA: Harvard University Press, 1993); Michelle Alexander, *The New Jim Crow: Mass Incarceration in the Age of Colorblindness* (New York:

The New Press, 2012); and Jill Leovy, *Ghettoside: A True Story of Murder in America* (London: Vintage, 2014).

Chapter 6: The global ghetto

There is a vast literature on the ghetto and global culture. Along with the references in this chapter and Chapter 5, see also Stephen Pimpare, *Ghettos, Tramps and Welfare Queens: Down and Out on the Silver Screen* (Oxford: Oxford University Press, 2017) and Robin D. G. Kelley, *Yo' Mamma's Disfunktional! Fighting the Cultural Wars in Urban America* (Boston: Beacon Press, 1997). See also http://genius.com/artists/Rap-genius/ for the huge number of rap songs which take the ghetto as their subject.

Index

For the benefit of digital users, indexed terms that span two pages (e.g., 52–53) may, on occasion, appear on only one of those pages

A

African-Americans 12–13, 88–117
  in Chicago 93–105
  in New York 105–13
Age of the Ghetto (1516–1789) 2, 14–38
Améry, Jean 81–2
Ancona 22, 24, 28–9, 31–2
Antin, Mary 59
antisemitism 12, 15–16, 62–6, 123–4
apartheid 119–20
Auerbach, Berthold 42
Auerbach, Rachel 78
Auschwitz-Birkenau 69, 73–4, 81, 87

B

Baldwin, James 88–90, 111
Baron, Salo 37–8
Bauman, Zygmunt 121, 124–5
Biebow, Hans 70–4
Black Arts Movement 112
Black Belts 90–6
black civil rights 13, 89–92, 102–3

Bonfil, Robert 38
Britain, imagined ghettos 50–4
Bronzeville 98–9, 103, 113–14
Browning, Christopher 75
bubonic plague (1630–1) 23
Budapest, Hungary 87

C

Cabrini-Green housing project 104
Cahan, Abraham 55–9
caricatures 115
Catholic Church 3–6, 8–10, 15–19, 24–6, 38
  counter-reformation (1545–1648) 16–17, 24, 37–8, 49
Cesarani, David 78–9
Chełmno death camp 72–3, 77–8
Chicago, USA 93–105
Chicago Freedom Movement (CFM) 102
civil rights 39
Clark, Kenneth 110–11
Cohen, Richard 42
Council of Basel (1434) 3
Council of Ten, Venice 18–19, 21–2

Cum Nimis Absurdum, papal bull (1955) 24, 26–9
Czerniaków, Adam 76, 78

D

death camps 72–3, 77–80, 83–7
deindustrialization 112–13, 115–16
Denmark 125–6
Drake, St Clair and Horace Clayton 94–8, 106, 113–14
Du Bois, W. E. B. 89, 96–7, 100–2, 123–5
Duneier, Mitchell 12–13

E

Ellison, Ralph 89, 111, 114
Everett, Percival 114–15
expansion of ghettos 20–2, 30–1, 36, 82–3, 91
expulsion of Jews 4–6, 14–15, 29–30, 33–4, 62, 72–3, 78, 84

F

Federal Housing Administration (FHA) 99
Final Solution 65, 73–5, 86
Florence, Italy 33–8
Fondaco dei Tedeschi 21–2
Fourth Lateran Council (1215) 3, 27
France, imagined ghettos 48–50
Frank, Hans 75
Frankfurt am Main, Germany 4–9, 14–15, 41–2, 52, 72
Franzos, Karl Emil 46–50
Freeman, Lance 91, 97, 99

G

gated communities 126
Gaza Strip 124–5

genocide 65–6, 72, 84–5, 87, 123–4
German-Jews 11–12, 41–4, 57, 61–2, 86, 95
German-Turks 125–6
Germany
  emancipation of Jews 40
  the Holocaust 65, 72–4, 84–5, 110, 123–4
  imagined ghettos 41–8
  Jewish quarters 4–11
Ghetto 1935 62–3
Ghetto Nuovissimo, Venice 9, 23, 36
Ghetto Nuovo, Venice 8–9, 19–21, 23
ghettos
  definition 1–2, 4–6, 60, 121
  imagined 9–11, 39–60
  origins 2–3, 8–9, 12–14, 19–21, 23, 30, 40, 91, 94–5, 109, 121–3
Ghetto Vecchio 21–2
Gill, Jonathan 107
Giuliani, Rudolph 112–13
Great Depression 91–2, 98–9, 105–7, 109
Great Migration (1916) 90–1, 94–5, 105–6
Gregorovius, Ferdinand 31–2
Greiser, Arthur 67–8, 70, 73

H

Hapgood, Hutchins 50–1, 59
Harlem ghetto 88–90, 105–13
Harlem Renaissance 107–9
Harlem Riot (1964) 111–12
Harrison, Hubert 105
Haynes, Bruce 93, 119
Hebraeorum Gens, papal bull (1569) 29, 33–4
Heine, Heinrich 41–2, 48
Henry Hormer homes 103–4
Heydrich, Reinhard 63–6, 72–5, 85–6

Hirsch, Arnold 99–100
Home Owners' Loan Corporation
    (HOLC) 99
Horthy, Miklós 87
Howells, Willian Dean 59
Hughes, Langston 107–8
Hutchinson, Ray 104–5, 119

I

Impey, Angela 119–20
Italy 6, 8–10, 14–38
    Age of the Ghetto (1516–1789) 2,
        14–17, 26, 37–9, 62, 125
    empires 14, 16–17
    Florentine ghetto 33–8
    Roman ghetto 24–33, 39
    Venetian Empire 18–24

J

January Uprising 80
jazz music 107–8, 114
Jenkins, Juanta Mae 114
Jewish Fighting Organisation
    (ŻOB) 79–82
Jewish Maxwell Street Ghetto 94–5
Jewish quarters 2–9, 37–8, 41–2,
    52, 121–3
    in United States 11–12, 54–60
Jews 5
    conversion 3, 14–15, 32–4
    emancipation 10–11, 39–40,
        43–4, 124
Judengasse (Jew's alley) 2–8,
    40–4, 52
Julius III (Pope) 28

K

Kaplan, Chaim 77
Kehillot Kadoshot (holy
    communities) 3, 9–11, 33,
    40–3, 53–4, 59

Kelley, Robin 115–16
Kerner Commission 102–3
King, Martin Luther Jr 89, 102
Kompert, Leopold 42–9, 53
Korczak, Janusz 78
Kristallnacht (night of broken
    glass) 64

L

Lazarus, Emma 55–7
League of Cambria 18
Levantines 16, 21–3, 35
Levi, Primo 69, 118–19
literature
    American 50–1, 54–60
    British 50–4
    French 48–50
    German 42–8
    about Harlem 107–8
Litzmannstadt 68–9, 71
Livorno, Italy 22, 28–9, 33–7
Locke, Alain 108–9
Łódź ghetto 66–74, 118–19
London ghetto, East End 51–2
Los Angeles riots (1965) 102

M

Magbane, Zine 120–1
Marranos (new Christians)
    22, 28–9
Mazower, Mark 87
Medici, Cosimo I de 33–4
Medici, Ferdinando de 33–6
Mendes, Dona Gracia 28–9
merchants 16–17, 21–4, 28–9, 35–8
Michman, Dan 65, 85
Miller, Wayne 59–60
Monti di Pietà 18, 24
Moses statue (Michelangelo) 25
Murray, Albert 110–11
Moynihan Report 114–15
Muslims 3–6, 14–15, 125–6

Napoleon Bonaparte 6-7, 10, 39
Nazism 12, 61-87, 110, 123-4
New Negros 108-9
New York ghetto, Lower East Side
    54-5, 57-60, 118-19
New York Times 54-6
Niggaz Wit Attitudes (NWA) 115-16
Nightingale, Carl 121
Nordau, Max 54
Nuremberg Racial Purity Laws
    (1935) 61-4

O

Ofosky, Gilbert 107
Operation Barbarossa 83-5
Oppenheim, Moritz Daniel 43
Ottoman Empire 2-3, 16-17,
    21-3, 28, 33
Oyneg Shabbos ('Sabbath Delight')
    77-8

P

Pacyga, Dominic 100
Palfinger, Alexander 71
Paul III (Pope) 28
Paul IV (Pope) 24, 26, 28-9
Phillips, Barnet 56-7
Piazza delle Cinque Scole 24
Pitigliano, Italy 35
Pius V (Pope) 29, 33
pogroms 52, 54-5
Polish-Jews 64, 66-82
Ponentines 16-17, 22-3, 28, 36
poverty 9, 12, 15, 18, 31-2, 37-8,
    56, 92-3, 98-9, 103-5, 112-14
    deliberate starvation 71, 74-7,
    84, 109, 115-16
Powell, James 111-12
Prague 4-6, 8-9, 14-15, 43-4,
    72, 109
Prinz, Joachim 62

rap culture 119-21
Ravid, Bernard 2, 4-6, 16
Red Army 83-7
Reguer, Sara 15
resistance groups 79-82
Riis, Jacob 59
Ringelblum, Emmanuel 77-9
riots 88-90, 92, 96, 102-3, 110-12
Robert Taylor Homes, Chicago
    99-101
Rodriguez, Daniel 21-2
Roman ghetto 61
Rome, Italy 24-33, 39
Roosevelt, Franklin D. 92, 99
Rosenfeld, Oskar 118-19
Roth, Henry 59-60
Rotham, E. Natalie 16-17
Rothberg, Michael 124
Rothschild, Meyer Amschel
    (Rothschild banking
    dynasty) 48-9
Ruderman, David 37-8
Rumkowski, Chaim 68-70, 72-4,
    76-8, 118

S

schlemiel (village idiot) 44-5
Schwartz, Daniel B 62-3
Sebald, W. G. 49-50
Segregation 1-2, 123-4
    of black Americans 12, 88-9,
    92-4, 96-7, 100-3, 106,
    110-12, 116-17, 119, 121-2
    of Jews 3-9, 16, 20, 32, 62
Sennett, Richard 15
Seraglio degli Hebrei (Enclosure of
    the Jews) 9, 26-7
Shelby, Tommie 115-17
Siena, Italy 33-5
Sixtus V (Pope) 30
slums 1, 30, 67-8, 88-91, 94-7,
    99-100, 103, 107, 112, 119

Soweto, South Africa 119–21, 123
Spain, Jewish populations
    2–6, 14–15
Speer, Albert 73
Stauben, Daniel 48–9
Stehle, Maria 125–6
Stroll, The 98

T

Talmud 7–8, 26
terra firma 18–19, 36
Theresienstadt 86–7
Third Lateran Council (1179) 3
travelling concepts 11–13
Treblinka death camp 72–3, 78–9

U

Übelhör, Friedrich 67–8
United States 88–117
    Jewish immigrants 11–12, 41,
        50–1, 54–6, 90–1
    literature 50–1, 54–60
USSR 82–7

V

Venice, Italy 8–9, 14–15, 18–25, 27,
    30–1, 98
Vogelstein, Herman 25, 61

W

Wacquant, Loïc 103, 113
walled communities 4–6,
    37–8, 68, 91
Wannsee Conference 72, 78, 85
Warsaw ghetto 74–82, 123–5
Warsaw Ghetto Uprising
    79–82, 89–90
Warthegau 64–8, 72
Weill, Alexandre 48
West, Cornel 115–16
Wilson, David 112–13
Wilson, William Julius 92–3
Winant, Howard 119
Wirth, Louis 93–5
World War I 59–60, 68, 90, 95,
    106–7, 118–19
World War II 12, 61–87, 90, 106, 124
Wright, Richard 98–9

Y

Yezierska, Anzia 59–60
Yiddish 10–11, 40, 44–5, 51, 56–8,
    62–3, 66

Z

Zangwill, Israel 11, 50–5,
    57–9

Index

ANTISEMITISM
A Very Short Introduction
Steven Beller

Antisemitism - a prejudice against or hatred of Jews - has been a chillingly persistent presence throughout the last millennium, culminating in the dark apogee of the Holocaust. This *Very Short Introduction* examines and untangles the various strands of antisemitism seen throughout history, from medieval religious conflict to 'new' antisemitism in the 21st century. Steven Beller reveals how the phenomenon grew as a political and ideological movement in the 19th century, how it reached it its dark apogee in the worst genocide in modern history - the Holocaust - and how antisemitism still persists around the world today.

www.oup.com/vsi

ARISTOCRACY
A Very Short Introduction
William Doyle

This short introduction shows how ideas of aristocracy originated in ancient times, were transformed in the Middle Ages, and have only fallen apart over the last two centuries. The myths in which aristocracies have always sought to shroud themselves are stripped away, but the true sources of their enduring power are also revealed. Their outlook and behaviour affected the rest of society in innumerable and sometimes surprising ways, but perhaps most surprising was the way in which a centuries-old aristocratic hegemony crumbled away over the last two hundred years. In this *Very Short Introduction* William Doyle considers why this happened and what remains today.

www.oup.com/vsi

CITIZENSHIP
A Very Short Introduction
Richard Bellamy

Interest in citizenship has never been higher. But what does it mean to be a citizen of a modern, complex community? Why is citizenship important? Can we create citizenship, and can we test for it? In this fascinating Very Short Introduction, Richard Bellamy explores the answers to these questions and more in a clear and accessible way. He approaches the subject from a political perspective, to address the complexities behind the major topical issues. Discussing the main models of citizenship, exploring how ideas of citizenship have changed through time from ancient Greece to the present, and examining notions of rights and democracy, he reveals the irreducibly political nature of citizenship today.

'Citizenship is a vast subject for a short introduction, but Richard Bellamy has risen to the challenge with aplomb.'

Mark Garnett, TLS

www.oup.com/vsi